The Parents' Practical Guide to

RESILIENCE

*for Children Aged 2–10
on the Autism Spectrum*

Illinois Early Intervention Clearinghouse
ECAP/ University of Illinois
20 Children's Research Center
51 Gerty Dr, Champaign, IL 61820
ILDS Delivery Code ZCH-iEiS

by the same authors

The Parents' Practical Guide to Resilience for Preteens and Teenagers on the Autism Spectrum
Jeanette Purkis and Emma Goodall
ISBN 978 1 78592 275 6
eISBN 978 1 78450 575 2

The Guide to Good Mental Health on the Autism Spectrum
Jeanette Purkis, Emma Goodall and Jane Nugent
Forewords by Wenn Lawson and Kirsty Dempster-Rivett
ISBN 978 1 84905 670 0
eISBN 978 1 78450 195 2

The Autism Spectrum Guide to Sexuality and Relationships
Understand Yourself and Make Choices that are Right for You
Emma Goodall
Forewords by Wenn Lawson and Jeanette Purkis
ISBN 978 1 84905 705 9
eISBN 978 1 78450 226 3

The Wonderful World of Work
A Workbook for Asperteens
Jeanette Purkis
ISBN 978 1 84905 499 7
eISBN 978 0 85700 923 4

Finding a Different Kind of Normal
Misadventures with Asperger Syndrome
Jeanette Purkis
ISBN 978 1 84310 416 2
eISBN 978 1 84642 469 4

of related interest

Parenting without Panic
A Pocket Support Group for Parents of Children and Teens on the Autism Spectrum (Asperger's Syndrome)
Brenda Dater
ISBN 978 1 84905 941 1
eISBN 978 0 85700 958 6

Helping Children with Complex Needs Bounce Back
Resilient Therapy™ for Parents and Professionals
Kim Aumann and Angie Hart
ISBN 978 1 84310 948 8
eISBN 978 1 84642 893 7

The Parents' Practical Guide to

RESILIENCE

*for Children Aged 2–10
on the Autism Spectrum*

Jeanette Purkis and Emma Goodall

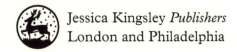
Jessica Kingsley *Publishers*
London and Philadelphia

First published in 2018
by Jessica Kingsley Publishers
73 Collier Street
London N1 9BE, UK
and
400 Market Street, Suite 400
Philadelphia, PA 19106, USA

www.jkp.com

Library of Congress Cataloging in Publication Data
A CIP catalog record for this book is available from the Library of Congress

British Library Cataloguing in Publication Data
A CIP catalogue record for this book is available from the British Library

ISBN 978 1 78592 274 9
eISBN 978 1 78450 574 5

Printed and bound in the United States

CONTENTS

CHAPTER 5 Common Issues for Autistic Children and Their Families between Ages Seven and Ten 131

INTRODUCTION

This book came about because Emma Goodall, one of the authors, heard the following story from the other author, Jeanette Purkis, and thought about it, in that very autistic way of revisiting and revisiting the story over and over. Emma then phoned Jeanette and said, 'I think we should write a workbook for parents, to teach their autistic children and teens to be resilient.'

In 2012, I met a young man who had been diagnosed with Asperger syndrome when he was 6 years old, Adam.[1] He was 21 when I met him. I told Adam that I was autistic and had written a book and that I worked full-time for the Australian Public Service. He responded almost immediately with, 'That's not true.' In Adam's universe, being autistic and writing books and working full-time was impossible. I spoke with him for a while. Adam had left school when he was 15. In the ensuing six years, he had not reconnected with education in any form. It was evident that, as far as Adam was concerned, education and work were for other people. He had never ridden on the bus and didn't have a driving licence, so presumably he had been driven to every place he ever went to by parents or friends of the family. He had spent his six years out of school playing computer games in his bedroom. His only social connection was to family. I spoke to Adam's parents and could almost physically feel their anxiety for their son. They also didn't seem to think he was capable of much else other than playing computer games. They had been told how he was going to live a limited life due to his autism by a range of educators and clinicians, and this seemed to have become a self-fulfilling prophecy. Independence and resilience were missing in Adam's life. He seemed to have been done a great disservice by two things that are all too prevalent for autistic young people – an assumption by a large section of society that autism is limiting and that autistic people are less able to function in society. This was combined with the understandable

---

1   Name changed.

anxiety of parents who have been told throughout their child's life about all the challenges and deficits that come with autism and few or none of the positives. I really felt for Adam and wanted to address this issue somehow, for surely there were many more autistic young people in a similar situation. (Jeanette Purkis)

Adam's story is one of the many things that inspired this book, as it caught Emma's attention due to her passion for ensuring that other autistics are on a path to a good life. The story demonstrates the need for resilience in autistic young people. Resilience is essential for navigating the adult world and being a fulfilled person who can reach their potential. Both Emma and Jeanette can be seen as successful autistic adults, in that they both work and live in their own homes (with fur and human family). However, underneath that veneer, both women are still autistic and still struggle with sensory and communication differences in a non-autistic world. It is their resilience and drive to make a difference that enable them to learn from mistakes and move forward, even if that learning can take decades at times!

One of the challenges around the autism diagnosis is that it can unintentionally lead to dependence and a lack of resilience and confidence in autistic children and young people, as is evident from Adam's story. The diagnosis – which should ideally be liberating and empower the autistic person to understand and value their unique experience of the world – can sometimes, sadly, result in dependence and disengagement. A focus on deficits and perceived incompetence and messages given to a child can result in autistic children and young people doubting themselves and being unable to take on challenges. Building independence and resilience is a great way to address this.

Several factors probably influenced Adam's challenges and lack of independence. Adam's story, however, is far from inevitable. Autistic children and young people have the capacity to be independent and resilient. Building resilience and independence in autistic children can start at a very young age. The earlier the process of building resilience starts, the better. This book aims to empower parents of autistic children to help them promote resilience in their child. Independence can be taken to mean able to live independently or requires support to live a fulfilling life. Being verbal is not a prerequisite for either of these, and many adults who do not use speech live happy and fulfilling lives.

If a parent thinks their child may be autistic, or even if they think they may not be, this book will be a useful tool for teaching resilience. All the activities are based on over fifteen years of teaching and education consultancy experience, as well as having been audited by a variety of different autistic adults and parents to ensure the activities are beneficial.

This book is a practical, activity-based resource for parents of autistic children aged between 2 and 10 years. It is focused on guiding parents to build the foundations of resilience and independence in their children. The book provides parents with information on resilience and the main developmental stages for children on the autism spectrum aged from 2–10 years of age. The book will take you through life events and milestones at different ages and identify where difficulties and barriers to resilience may arise and how to address them. Each life event will include exercises that you can work through in order to more effectively build resilience and independence in your child. The information will help you understand what your child might be experiencing so as to enable you to better assist them through their life journey.

This book aims to enable you to promote resilience in your child. It is written from a strengths-based approach to autism and the view that autistic people interpret and engage with the world in a way that is different rather than deficient. Building resilience can set up autistic children to navigate through life better and build their self-esteem and confidence. Resilience building at young ages can have a significant impact on children's ability to successfully navigate life in adulthood and will help them to find their place in society and reach their potential as adults when the time comes.

The book will take you through what resilience is, why it is needed, what the risk factors and protective factors are around resilience in children on the autism spectrum, as well as the challenges for children on that spectrum. It will work through a number of life events that children generally experience, including trying new foods, visiting relatives, meeting other children, going to pre-school, managing being told 'No!', sharing with others, going to the doctor, learning new motor skills, starting school, changes at school, social interactions, losing a game, responding resiliently to bullying, going to the dentist, sleepovers, school camp and managing emotional distress.

Each life event will include helpful information and activities to enable you to guide your child through the event successfully and build their strength and confidence. The book will include information on how to ascertain where the child is at in terms of their resilience. There are also performance indicators showing what a good outcome at each life stage might look like for your child. There is also a chapter on failing successfully. Being able to manage failure is an essential life skill for everyone, and particularly for autistic kids who may be anxious around failure and mistakes.

Meltdowns and shutdowns are mentioned throughout this book. An autistic meltdown or shutdown occurs when an autistic person is overloaded, either with emotions, social input, sensory stimuli, anxiety or other overwhelming experiences. A shutdown is an internalising response to being overwhelmed and a meltdown is an externalising response. Both of these are unintentional behaviour, which is almost impossible to control. Autistic people – including children – do not have meltdowns intentionally, and they generally feel very bad that a meltdown has occurred. Meltdowns and shutdowns are very different from a tantrum, which occurs when a child wants their own way but is not being allowed to have their own way.

While some of the events in this book list decreasing meltdowns as an indicator that your child is doing well, it does not follow that a meltdown is poor behaviour. A meltdown is an indicator of overload rather than poor behaviour. Building resilience and confidence in an ever-increasing range of environments and activities helps to minimise the frequency of autistic meltdowns. Over time, many autistics develop the ability to cope with new or challenging situations, with resultant meltdowns happening later when the autistic is in a safe place, such as at home after school or work. However, without resilience and confidence, even adults struggle to manage their meltdowns.

Punishing or fixating on meltdowns is unlikely to help your child address their challenges and may, in fact, be counterproductive. If your child is experiencing fewer meltdowns, it is an indication that they are managing life events better. This is a very positive indicator of their ability to manage long term.

CHAPTER 1

RESILIENCE AND AUTISTIC CHILDREN

An Overview

WHAT IS RESILIENCE?

When used to describe people, resilience is defined as: *the ability to recover readily from illness, depression, adversity, or the like; buoyancy.*[1] Resilience is essentially the capacity to 'bounce back' fairly quickly after a difficulty or adverse experience. Resilience basically involves working through any challenges or difficulties encountered in a proactive manner that will enable you to build confidence and mastery in overcoming that difficulty. Through doing this, a person can build mastery and confidence in other areas of their life, without even realising that they are doing so.

People who do not often have to face adversity or overcome challenges do not have the opportunities to develop resilience and are more likely to struggle long term with even minor difficulties than people who have developed resilience as they have grown up. This means that parents, families and educators all have roles to play in helping children experience, manage and overcome difficulties in ways that naturally scaffold the development of resilience.

Resilient people tend to be more able to face and overcome challenges and disappointment with positive outcomes in terms of personal growth and mental health. They tend to be more confident and willing to take on new activities and challenges and less anxious about change. The act of overcoming or managing a difficulty often gives people the confidence and skills to take on and overcome further challenges in life. Resilience impacts on a person's sense of self-worth and self-esteem. It is a key skill for living and is an important protective factor for mental health and well-being.

---

1   Source: www.dictionary.com/browse/resilience (accessed 23 October 2016).

Resilience is in a sense a self-replicating skill. For example, once a child has resiliently managed a challenging situation, they will most likely be more confident about their ability to overcome other challenges that they might encounter. This means that having resilience facilitates confidence, skills and attitudes, which feed into a person's ability to take on challenges, which in turn can mean those challenges are less traumatic. This means people are more confident about their capacity to take on difficulties and less worried about their ability to deal with what challenges the future might hold. This in turn gives the person confidence and their ability to be resilient increases.

Resilience is a key life skill for everyone, including, or perhaps especially, autistic people. This book is written from the insider or lived-experience perspectives of the autism spectrum by two adults who have had very different but equally successful resilience journeys. In other words, both authors have built up enough resilience that they are able to manage the challenges that they face in life, both big and little, in ways that enable them to live as successful autistics who are comfortable in themselves.

This book aims to impart information that will enable parents, educators and other caregivers to facilitate the development of resilience in all the keys areas that young autistic children need in order to successfully set up these children for meeting the challenge of their adolescence.

WHAT IMPEDES RESILIENCE?

Resilience can be difficult to attain. A number of factors can impede or make it difficult to acquire resilience. These include:

- *Invalidation.* Invalidation refers to situations where a person's identity, self, safety, experience or beliefs are invalidated by others. Invalidating experiences can include bullying, abuse, violence, discrimination, 'gaslighting' or bigotry and vilification. At its most simple, invalidation is the statement, 'You can't,' where a validating statement that could be used instead would be, 'You are learning how to' or 'I am learning how to teach you,' or at the very least, 'You can't yet.' Even when it seems highly unlikely that someone will ever be able to do a particular thing, say, for example, be a brain surgeon (for a person with no depth perception this would seem to be highly unlikely), to deny the opportunity is invalidating, whereas to explain the skills a person would need to acquire in order to become a brain surgeon may drive the ambition and persistence required. Autistic children, young people and adults often experience invalidation. Invalidation impacts on self-image and self-esteem. Acquiring resilience requires a degree of self-confidence and positive self-esteem, which invalidation strips away from a person, leaving them less able to take on the skill.

- *An assumption of incompetence.* Assumptions of incompetence are often directed at autistic people. This can take a variety of forms and include the idea that autistic people are not able to make decisions on their own behalf, live independently, work, have friendships or relationships, raise children and a variety of other assumptions. For autistic children it can mean their capacity to learn, play, communicate and interact socially is questioned and dismissed. Assuming incompetence is in effect invalidating and disabling of a person. A simple example is dressing yourself. A child who has been assumed to be incapable of dressing themselves will not be given the opportunity to do so and therefore will not learn to do so. In this way, people can begin to think that their assumption of incompetence was correct as it can become a negative and damaging self-fulfilling prophecy that disables children and young people.

- *Paternalism/shielding from difficulties.* This is a less obvious issue, but one that hinders the development of resilience and can also prevent people from achieving their potential. In some instances, people who are caring for or about someone can have low expectations of that person's capability to do things which others take for granted. This attitude of shielding people from challenges or difficulties can be seen in parents and carers trying to protect their children from short-term or long-term pain or hardship. Many autistic people, and autistic children and young people especially, have experienced this. However, even if the child or young person feels loved and protected, as a result paternalism can lead to the child/young person losing confidence in their capacity to do things. Self-doubt impedes the capacity to be resilient.

- *Negative messaging about who you are.* Negative messaging is a part of invalidation and gaslighting but also a key aspect of prejudice. Messaging about who you are impacts on your sense of self in relation to others. For example, a New Zealander is seen differently in New Zealand to Australia, where the messaging about what it means to be a New Zealander is quite different to 'back home'. Autistic people often go through their lives only being told negative things about themselves and autism in general – not only from bullies but also in some instances from carers, educators, other professionals and sometimes even their parents. A child who has only been told what they can't do often internalises the message and this leads to difficulty in acquiring resilience. Autism being perceived only in terms of deficits rather than strengths can compound this, just as a child internalising racist attitudes would perceive their ethnicity differently to a child who internalised more positive messages about their heritage.

- *Previous failure.* This can be both a learning tool and/or an impediment to developing resilience. A history of failing at an activity, particularly when the mistake is emphasised and focused on by adult role models or important peers can have a negative impact on resilience. The failure can become a traumatic memory, making it almost impossible for the child to try that activity again. This can be compounded by negative responses to the failure, which denigrate the child instead of putting the failure into perspective and encouraging them to move on. In the same way that overcoming one challenge can promote ongoing resilience in different areas of life, this kind of trauma relating to failure can result in flow-on effects to other activities, making the person less likely to attempt not only the activity that they failed at but also other activities. However, where the failure is used as a non-judgemental discussion point to evaluate possible future responses to a similar situation, it can support the development of resilience.

- *Perfectionism.* Perfectionism often results in a high level of anxiety and fear of failure around a specific activity as the child or person seeks to complete the activity perfectly. Perfectionism can actually prevent a person from attempting the activity in the first place due to their anxiety that they will be unable to do the activity well enough, or if they do start, it can impede them from completing what they are doing in case it 'isn't good enough'. Perfectionism makes it very hard to build resilience and can often be mistaken for work avoidance or bad behaviour, for example, when a child tears up their written work in class because the letters are not formed 'perfectly'.

WHY DO AUTISTIC CHILDREN NEED RESILIENCE?

While resilience is a valuable skill for everybody, autistic people, and children in particular, have a great need to acquire resilience in order to achieve their own personal potential and maximise their well-being. First, autistic people face specific challenges that can set them back in terms of confidence and self-worth. They may find navigating the largely non-autistic world frightening, anxiety-provoking and invalidating. Autistic children can struggle to communicate their needs. Some may be non-verbal for part or all of the time and, while there are communication methods and devices available, it can take some years for the child to be given such invaluable tools. Even autistic children who speak can struggle to understand and explain their needs. Change or a lack of predictability can be overwhelming. The idea of doing new things for autistic children – whatever those may be – can induce meltdowns and shutdown. Given these considerations, the attribute of resilience, which allows a child to be more confident in the face of adversity and change, is particularly important to acquire.

Without resilience, children can go through life finding things increasingly challenging and becoming more and more anxious about taking on new activities. They may become autistic young adults who cannot engage with society, leading to wasted potential for that person and the wider world. Their anxiety will increase exponentially, whereas with the development of resilience, anxiety may not cease but it will peak and trough with lower and less frequent peaks.

Instilling resilience and independence skills early on in a child's development can address many issues and promote the ability to take on – and succeed at – new challenges.

HOW CAN RESILIENCE CHANGE YOUR CHILD'S LIFE FOR THE BETTER?

Resilience is helpful for autistic children in a number of ways, including:

- helping them to navigate through life's milestones in a positive manner which promotes growth and knowledge

- building their self-confidence and self-esteem

- enabling them to build a strong, positive self-identity

- helping them manage change and/or unpredictability

- helping them recover from setbacks and disappointments

- helping to reduce stress, overload, and meltdown and shutdown

- helping them to succeed in challenges and also to accept and learn from mistakes or failures

- helping them to understand the need for practice and patience to develop a new skill

- laying the foundations for life as an independent adult, whether or not they require a lot or only a little assistance in that life

- helping them to understand social–emotional boundaries and limits and work within those

- assisting in social interactions with difficult peers

- fostering a genuine sense of place in the world (belonging in the widest sense of the word) and thus removing the need for acceptance by any peer group in order to feel they belong

- building confidence in taking on challenges

- providing them with a solid base to move forward from childhood into teenage years and adulthood.

HOW DOES A PERSON ACQUIRE RESILIENCE?

Resilience is a skill that is essentially acquired through experience. Practice makes perfect when building resilience and independence skills. Every skill that a child acquires can be seen in terms of them building their skills incrementally. For autistic children, these skills may sometimes take longer to develop and require a greater degree of support from parents and educators. If autistic children are adequately prepared for a new life experience, they are more likely to pass through it with more confidence and proficiency, meaning it will be less likely to be traumatic.

In this way, building mastery of one experience or life stage is likely to flow onto other events or skills. Embedding resilience skills started young can scaffold that child's development. It is likely to result in a greater degree of confidence in adulthood.

The key to building resilience for anybody is to face challenges and difficulties and overcome them. Of course, some things that potentially build resilience can also result in trauma and heightened anxiety and other mental health difficulties. No parent would want their child exposed to that. The key to building resilience with children and young people – including those on the autism spectrum – is to introduce a series of controlled challenges to help them incrementally take on slightly larger challenges and build their resilience.

Setting out to develop resilience is like setting out to run a marathon. Although you could just get up one day and run a marathon, this is the most risky and problematic way to approach the goal. Instead, most people would increase their fitness and stamina over time by running short distances and increasing the time and distance they run as they feel more confident and successful.

It can help to view resilience as a muscle that can be developed and grown through the 'exercise' of taking on new challenges. As the child masters one challenge, they will ideally build their strength to take on the next. For this to be effective and supportive, there are a few considerations to take into account, which will be covered later in this book.

Often parents – and particularly parents of children on the autism spectrum – are very reluctant to expose their child to difficulty in any way, shape or form. They may not want to expose their child to the possibility of failure or disappointment and may be highly protective of their child. While noble and understandable, autistic people – and all people –

experience challenges, setbacks and failings throughout their life. For an autistic child who is likely to be acutely sensitive around failure or setbacks, building resilience through dealing with challenges can be a very good thing. If you imagine that a child is shielded from difficulty until they move out of home at the age of 25, for example, how much more is a setback or error going to impact on them than if they were a small child started off with small, controlled challenges delivered by supportive parents and/or carers? There are a number of points in this process that parents may find hard to navigate. One of the aims of this book is to better equip parents with the knowledge of when and how to introduce challenges in their child's life that are supportive and build resilience rather than producing trauma and angst.

It may be helpful for parents/carers to understand that many autistic adults ascribe their ability to manage as well as they do in life to being resilient, and that having parents who expected them to manage and overcome challenges from early childhood is key to that resilience. Autistic adults who struggle more with life and who are less resilient have often experienced lives that did not support the development of resilience, but were instead invalidating and assuming of long-term incompetence.

WHAT CHALLENGES TO RESILIENCE DO AUTISTIC CHILDREN TEND TO FACE?

Autistic people can face many barriers and challenges in relation to navigating the world, whether or not these are obvious to casual observers. This is true for autistic children and adults. It is also true for autistic people considered to have high support needs and also for those with apparently less need for support. When it comes to resilience, autistic children may have a range of significant barriers. If they have been raised with routines, they may be severely resistant to change in routine in a number of domains. These autistic children often find anything that upsets their routine traumatic, and such interruptions to the status quo can result in meltdown and/or shutdown. Helping autistic children manage change through predictability means that there is less anxiety about change. Autistic adults and young people who do not find change particularly difficult are clear that this is the case for predictable change, whereas unpredictable things can still provoke anxiety and require a degree of resilience. Autistic children and adults often have a number of attributes that make acquiring resilience very difficult. These include:

- lack of, or difficulty in acquiring self-awareness and insight

- challenges communicating and/or articulating their needs

- significant anxiety, frequently to the level of diagnosable clinical anxiety disorders or other mental health issues

- traumatic memories around difficulties or adversity in the past

- an assumption of incompetence from support people and family members

- poor self-esteem

- negative messaging from a large range of quarters, including the media and more personally; other children – bullies particularly – but also potentially clinicians and support people and even family members

- a lack of autism knowledge among people involved in the child's life.

Given that resilience is basically a skill that centres on successfully moving through new challenges and difficulties, it would appear that autistic children and young people are probably going to really struggle with developing resilience. Autistic children certainly tend to face more difficulties, and indeed barriers, than their non-autistic peers in building their resilience. However, this is precisely the reason why autistic children *need* resilience skills. Gaining resilience is likely to address a number of the risk factors listed here. It may be a more difficult journey but that is precisely why it is so important to promote resilience and independence among autistic kids. The purpose of building resilience and independence skills in autistic children is to set them up for a life where they can address difficulties and adversity and in doing so live a more fulfilled and enjoyable life. No two children will have the same resilience journey and it is important to understand that resilience in one aspect of challenge or adversity may not automatically translate to another area. So, for example, a child may be resilient in terms of managing challenges around eating in the home, but not yet around food in other environments.

LAYING THE FOUNDATIONS OF RESILIENCE AND INDEPENDENCE FOR AUTISTIC CHILDREN

Positive experiences and achieving success can lay the foundations of resilience for young kids. Feeling more relaxed and confident – and, importantly, avoiding major trauma or severe anxiety – puts a child in a frame of mind that is more conducive to taking on new challenges and, through this, building resilience. If a child's life is experienced as being predominantly stressful and frightening, this can feed into fear of taking on any new challenges.

Building resilience needs to start from a solid base. A child needs to have a place they can go to – physically or through their imagination and memory – where they feel safe, supported and have some sense of control and agency. Parents can help create this kind of environment for their child. Self-confidence and, through it, resilience often begins when the child has their own 'place of safety'. Think about the times when you, as an adult, are prepared to take risks or confidently face challenges. Most people are more confident when surrounded by people who believe in them and when they have a positive sense of self and a belief in themselves as capable people. These things are in themselves a 'place of safety'. Ideally, this place of safety that is established in the home can be extended from home to the school environment, with the classroom teacher being a strong support.

For autistic children, a safe and predictable home environment can be instrumental in boosting their self-confidence and a sense of consistency. This does not mean that these children need strict routines, rather that they always know what is happening now as well as what will be happening next, whether this is because they are reliably informed or because there are rhythms and routines that they have learnt.

In addition, autistic children can be highly attuned to conflict and anger, as well as changes in the environment. It should be noted that what is a predictable environment is not the same for each child or family. Most parents, however, will be aware of their child feeling that the home environment is lacking in consistency or security through observing differences in their behaviour. For some autistic children, changing the living room rug without pre-warning them will be perceived as devastating, but to others it will not matter. However, letting children know about or even being actively involved in changes in their own environment is conducive to creating that 'place of safety'.

All children, and especially autistic children, do well in an environment of love and trust, where interactions are respectful and there is little conflict. Autistic children, including those who are non-verbal, often have a high level of sensitivity to the emotions of those around them. Things like anger and frequent conflict can be incredibly traumatic for a child on the spectrum. If the child themselves is on the receiving end of anger and blame, this will undermine their sense of a 'place of safety'. Autistics can assume that they are to blame when there are strong negative emotions around them, even when they are not, so it is important to teach autistic children about the experiences and roles of these emotions in the lives of those around them in an honest and open way. Couples do argue from time to time. It does not necessarily mean that violence will ensue or that the couple will split up. Sometimes arguing is just a means to settling issues and working through difficulties. It is important to make your child aware that arguments and conflict between parents do occur from time to time but it does not mean that they will split up. As many autistic children internalise parental arguing and feel somehow to blame, it is important to let them know it isn't their fault and neither is it their responsibility to 'fix' any issues between their parents.

A child may assume their teacher is angry with them, if their teacher is angry, even if the teacher smiles at them. Whereas, if the teacher tells the children that an incident on the way to school made them angry and they are trying to manage their anger, which is not any of the children's fault, the autistic child can learn that not all anger is directed at or blamed on them, as well as seeing that not all anger is destructive either.

Unplanned/unexplained changes to the physical environment can also be traumatic for many autistic children. Parents should be aware that moving a piece of furniture or carrying out renovations to the home can cause significant anxiety. A home environment where the child is supported and trusted is very important. However, autistic children who grow up with continual changes in the home environment or repeated house moving can become accustomed to this and view it as 'normal':

Leo is autistic and moved house a large number of times as a child. When he was about 25, Leo was asked if he minded moving house so much. Leo had no idea why someone would have a problem moving house. 'You pack your stuff in boxes, put it in a van, and then the van takes it to your new house. Then you unpack it. No different to changing classrooms at school over the summer holidays, except at school you carried a box and didn't need a van.'

Understanding your child and where they are coming from will not only improve your child's sense of consistency and security, it will most likely improve the relationships and dynamic in the family. When any child, but especially an autistic child is criticised for something they do not understand or perceive as fair criticism, it can be devastating and impedes the development of resilience.

There is an assumption that parents automatically know and understand their own children better than anyone else, but some non-autistic parents can feel that their autistic child is so different from them that they are unknowable. Despite this fear, understanding their autistic child is entirely possible for a non-autistic parent. It is important for parents and others to really get to know the child whilst developing an understanding as it can be very easy to misinterpret autistics and misunderstand autistic communication and behaviours.

There is a large variety of literature and videos where autistic adults, and in some cases children, talk about what it is like to be autistic. Non-autistic parents can start to learn about their child and his or her motivation and approach to life by looking at this information by autistic adults discussing their experiences. Using this background material in combination with non-judgemental observations of exactly what the child is doing is the key to knowing and understanding the child.

Another strategy for understanding your autistic child is to ask them why they did this or that thing and by taking an interest in the games and stories and other interests they may have. Asking why may not always elicit a response, or an expected answer, but if the question is genuine and non-judgemental, over time the responses will become more enlightening for the person asking. Autistic children are often highly sensitive to criticism and so will evade answering or answering truthfully if they are worried about further annoying, angering or upsetting the person asking.

The notion that autistic people are an unfathomable puzzle is unhelpful to both parents and autistic children. Having parents understand them is a great contributor to the place of safety for autistic children and adults. It also means that children are more likely to feel confident enough to raise issues they are having at school or other places, which can assist parents to act and address any issues.

It is important to remember that *all* people are individuals and that no two autistics are exactly alike. Motivations and behaviours are likewise individual, as the next scenario demonstrates:

I used to collect pencils and pens at school. I liked the way they looked and the way that no two had exactly the same visual textures on them. I got into trouble once when a teacher got really angry with me and asked me why I was stealing someone's pencil. I really had no idea what she was talking about, I never stole anything. I picked up the pens and pencils that people left behind on the floor or the desk, when they left the classroom. Sometimes, I found them on the floor in front of the lockers or on the gym change-room floor, but I never took them from anyone. But, when I said I hadn't stolen the pencil, the teacher opened my bag and grabbed a particular pencil, telling me that it belonged to another girl, and then I just couldn't hear any more except loud angry noises. I still don't know why I got in trouble. If that girl knew I had found her pencil, why didn't she just come and ask for it back? I would have given it to her. (Kate)

DEFICITS THINKING AND SELF-CONFIDENCE

One thing that needs to start as early as possible is supporting and promoting your child's self-confidence and positive sense of self. Resilience and self-confidence are strongly linked. Negative thinking and deficits thinking are prevalent around autism, with children more likely to hear what autistics can't do than what they can do. This is far from ideal. Giving a child negative reinforcement about their capabilities and skills, and focusing on what they can't do, can become a self-fulfilling prophecy; whereas, children who do not know that people assume they can't do something are far more likely to be able to do that thing. An interesting example of this relates to early childhood education. In the Montessori education system, young children learn very complex and complicated things such as the Latin name for leaf shapes and the mathematical names of two-dimensional and three-dimensional shapes. However, these types of concepts are assumed by other types of education systems to be far too complex for young children, who are therefore not introduced to them, and therefore cannot tell you that a ball is indeed a sphere or that a box is a rectangular prism. I am sure that if any pre-school assumed children could learn these things and are therefore taught them, the children would learn, just as they do in the Montessori system.

A number of negative views around autism are prevalent at the moment, as seen in the media and in the plethora of fundraising adverts for autism not-for-profit organisations, which stress the difficulties faced by autistics and do not mention the strengths and benefits of autism (of which there are undoubtedly both). Autistic adults face negative views and discrimination in employment, autistic parents have their parenting skills questioned, autistic students fail subjects at school due to their divergent learning styles not being understood, media articles on autism often focus entirely on the disability aspect and see autism as a tragedy or curse. Put all those things together and you get a world in which autistic children grow up and take those sorts of attitudes on board. You end up with autistic young adults who are convinced their experience is 'wrong' when in fact it is often just a bit different. With the right understanding and circumstances, that autistic child can live a successful and fulfilled life, but it is hard to do that if your belief about yourself is focused almost entirely on what you apparently can't do:

> I have lots of sensory issues, and so I can't drive. I have been very surprised to meet so many other autistic adults who do drive. I asked one once, how she had learnt to drive, and she said that she was not very good, but that it seemed to her that most drivers were not very good, so she had just had more lessons until she passed her test. She didn't know why I thought autistics couldn't drive, but I thought we couldn't because it is so hard for us to filter and process all the sensory input. (Barry)

For these reasons, parents starting out their child's path through life with positive reinforcement and support to scaffold new skill/knowledge development rather than deficits thinking can make a huge difference. Deficits thinking can have a number of unintended negative impacts. For example, it can result in a child being unwilling or unable to stand up to bullies or report bullying or other issues at school to a teacher or parent, as they see themselves as being 'weird' or somehow less valuable than their peers. It can also result in children being unwilling to try new things because they are sure that they will be hopeless at it, so why try.

Resilience grows from confidence. It is hard to embrace a place of safety when you are being constantly told that the way you experience life is wrong. A strengths focus is one important way to counter this:

> I wanted to learn to sail, I don't know why, but I really wanted to. My school had a sailing club with these tiny little one- and two-person boats that they took out onto the lake at the weekend. I signed up for the sailing club, even though I was not a particularly good swimmer. They said I could join the club as long as I could recover from a forced capsize in the swimming pool. They had every belief that I could do it, and talked me through what to do and how to do it. I couldn't do it because I panicked too much, but I will never forget that the teachers and other students believed in me and said I could come back and try again any time I wanted to. I can sort of paddle a canoe or kayak now, though I am not exactly good at it! (Mia)

UNDERSTANDING BEHAVIOURS

Autistic children are still children – they make mistakes and do things they aren't meant to. Autistic children can show poor behaviour and bad judgement, just like any other child. However, it is important to know what behaviour is unintentional, what is maladaptive and therefore reinforcing of unhelpful behaviour and what is deliberate naughtiness. One thing a lot of autistic people do that is often misunderstood is 'stimming'. Stimming is a term to describe any of a number of repetitive behaviours, involving movement or sound, which autistic people do to help regulate sensory or emotional issues. Stims can include things like hand flapping, spinning in a chair, chewing on a toy, coughing repeatedly or looking at sparkly things. Stimming generally makes autistic people feel better and is used consciously or subconsciously to help regulate emotions and maintain calm or seek a sense of joy or pleasure. To some non-autistic people, though, stimming can look odd. *All* people stim, it is just that tapping your fingers or twirling your hair is not labelled as a stim if you are non-autistic!

There are many resources for parents out there that say stimming – in any form – is poor behaviour and should be eradicated. It isn't, and it shouldn't be. Some people have stims that cause self-injury, and these need to be addressed, but with most stims, the main 'problem' is judgemental people. Self-injurious stims are not usually designed to self-harm in the way most people understand it. It is more that these stims help the autistic child or person to know that they exist. These types of stims are most common when an autistic child or person is still developing their interoceptive awareness, which is their ability to sense themselves. Specifically teaching interoception is an important part of supporting an autistic child or young person not to engage in behaviours that appear to be self-injurious.

When non-self-injurious activities like stimming are discouraged, this can be very unhelpful and damaging to self-worth and self-confidence. In addition, autistics *need* to stim, to help manage their emotions, so they will replace a 'forbidden' stim with another behaviour that may be even less desirable.

To think about the role of stimming as a self-calming activity, imagine that drinking coffee or tea, or even water, is suddenly labelled as a stim. Every time you reach for a drink, for example, on your way to work, or at your breaks, you are seen to be stimming and stared at, or even told off. Now, imagine how frustrated and grumpy you might be, if you were told that you are never allowed to drink tea or coffee again (and for those of you who don't drink those now, that you are not allowed to drink water except when it is given to you)!

EXERCISE – STIMMING

Imagine you are a young child, and that there is one thing that makes you feel calm when you are stressed. If you tap your leg with both your hands repeatedly, you feel better. One day, your teacher sees this and tells you to stop it. You don't know what you have done wrong. You haven't hurt anyone or damaged school property. Every time you try to soothe yourself by tapping your leg, you get told off. That makes you stressed but you can't do your best strategy for stress because your teacher's response to you doing that is the reason you are stressed! You don't know how to de-escalate stress, and you think that there must be something wrong with you:

- How does the teacher's attitude around your stimming impact on your attitudes about school?

- How is this disciplining of your stims likely to impact on how you address anxiety in the future? Remember how you would feel if you were told you were not allowed to have a drink of coffee ever again!

Modifying certain behaviours – like stimming, not making eye contact or lining up toys – can be extremely traumatic for the child and is often more focused on making them seem outwardly more non-autistic rather than doing anything to assist them to navigate the world. Unfortunately, when a child is traumatised by behaviour modification, it can have long-term ramifications, even impacting negatively on self-esteem, mental health and relationships with others. An example is insisting that autistic children make eye contact in cultures where eye contact during conversation is perceived as signalling attention to the speaker. In these cultural contexts, there is a widespread view that making eye contact during conversation is natural and all people do it, and not making eye contact represents poor communication. In fact, this is not really true. Making eye contact is a cultural consideration rather than an absolute value. In many cultures – including some Indigenous Australian cultures – making eye contact is considered aggressive and rude. In other cultures, eye contact by children to adults is viewed as disrespectful.

Many autistic people find eye contact invasive and feel extremely uncomfortable doing it. Some report that it is like lasers boring into their face or sharp knives stabbing at their eyes. Others report that it is too close and personal, conveying too much information and too many feelings, and that it is overwhelming to look in the eyes of another person. For these autistics, it can be impossible to listen to someone if they are required to make eye contact as the eye contact uses up all their available sensory and emotional processing!

The sorts of behaviour modification techniques used to make autistic children more socially appropriate are often getting them to do things that are unpleasant and largely unnecessary in terms of giving them useful skills for life. For example, imagine insisting on eye contact before every action, activity or communication, if that eye contact makes the child feel like they are having knives stabbed into their eyes. This child may end up associating all those activities with pain, too.

So, while behaviours that cause or will cause the child problems in the future do need addressing, many of the things autistic kids do 'wrong' are in fact just different. It is hard to be in a place of safety when your way of approaching the world is questioned and punished. Forcing a child to change behaviour that is, in fact, assisting them to feel safe and calm tends to be counterproductive, and will, in fact, almost certainly decrease their self-confidence and other attitudes and behaviours that encourage and support resilience.

THE VALUE OF TEACHING RESILIENCE EARLY

Autistic people who have been brought up with a very strict routine can struggle to manage change. Habits and responses formed in early childhood can dictate the habits and responses of a lifetime. Resilience can also become a habit, albeit a useful one. This is one of the key reasons for teaching resilience early.

Autistic children can experience many challenges and triggers and be highly anxious in relation to a number of things, including changes in routine and new and unfamiliar environments. They may experience extreme frustration due to an inability to communicate verbally or in difficulties articulating their needs and being understood by those around them. They may be strongly averse to certain sensory stimuli, or may be 'sensory seekers', being desperate not to leave an environment that causes sensory joy and stimulation. They may act in ways that – while meaningful to them – will confuse or upset their parents. They can engage in self-injurious stims and/or experience extreme meltdowns. It is important not to forget that all young children can struggle to make themselves understood to adults and experience issues around dealing with change as well, but for autistic children it can be that much more difficult. Another thing that autistic children experience is non-autistic people – including in some instances their parents or siblings – not understanding their needs due to differences between autistic and non-autistic communication and the prevalent view that the way autistic people communicate is 'wrong'. Some practices described as autism 'therapies' for young children, including those that try to make the child do things like making eye contact or stopping them from stimming, instead of being supportive, can be very stressful for autistic children and, contrary to the stated intention of the therapy, in fact be counterproductive to the child's development. We know this to be true from the writings of autistic adults, particularly from the USA, detailing how these experiences felt to them, and the lasting impact of this on their lives.

Taking all of those challenges into consideration, it would seem that encouraging and promoting resilience for young children on the autism spectrum is a good idea. One point to consider around this is the rights of the autistic child to be supported as their autistic self and not forced or coerced into behaving more 'non-autistic' where possible. It is important to realise that people can live well as autistic people, they are not 'fixed' autistics, and that how their autism presents will vary from day to day and context to context, just like your child's. Early intervention and therapy for autistic children, including the resilience techniques described in this book, should be aimed at addressing difficulties the child experiences in living their life well and becoming a content and fulfilled adult. Barriers to success need to be overcome or worked around, using the child's strengths, skills and interests to support them to learn new skills and understandings of the world around them.

While there are some significant issues which autistic children may face that require support to address or even change, being encouraged to change simply so that the child looks 'less autistic' to others, is generally quite unhelpful. Efforts would be better spent assisting the child with challenges like managing change, understanding and regulating their own emotions, communicating effectively (including with non-speech tools like picture exchange communication system or PECS) and developing their character, their sense of identity and their self-worth.

SUCCESSFULLY CONVEYING CONCEPTS AROUND RESILIENCE TO CHILDREN

While children might struggle to comprehend abstract concepts, this is no reason to avoid having conversations around resilience with them. Children can surprise us with their ability to grasp ideas and develop new skills. With all children, but especially autistic children, the key is to base the conversation around things that are meaningful to the child. For example, if the child has an interest in Thomas the Tank Engine, you might be able to work in a story about their favourite Thomas character dealing with something difficult and then refer that back to the child and relate it to something they are struggling with at the present time.

A key to conveying ideas around resilience and independence is to understand your child really well. You probably do already, but even so, have a think about what is important to them and has a big impact on their life. With young children, it is probably not a good idea to sit them down and have a conversation around what resilience and independence mean and how you are going to assist them to be more resilient. Instead, understanding their interests and what motivates them is a great way to understand where they are 'at', what is important to them and how you can think creatively and use your child's interests and likes to motivate them.

The key concepts to convey to children around resilience are:

- If something seems difficult, that is not a reason not to do it.

- You will be able to overcome difficulties, with some help.

- It is rarely possible to master a skill straight away. Practice actually does make perfect. Don't give up trying just because it is difficult to master.

- When trying something new, it is always okay to ask a parent or trusted adult to assist.

- Overcoming something difficult will make you feel really good and will mean you can do that thing again in the future and it will probably be easier.

- Competition is okay and it is also okay if you don't win.

- If you don't get it right the first time, that is okay.

You may like to complete this section to help you scaffold some of the conversations that you plan to have with your child.

My child's:

Favourite	Least favourite/most disliked/feared
animal	animal
character	character
toy	toy
song/story	song/story
activity	activity
person	person
thing	thing

Building in some initial controlled challenges to promote resilience may work very well if based in your child's passion or ('special') interest as they are very likely to have confidence in their ability to do that and they find activities around that area enjoyable. Understanding your child's passions and interests also has a nice unintended benefit for parents: that of understanding their child better. In this way, it can promote closer relationships between parents and children, particularly if everyone can work/play alongside or with each other, sharing an activity and so sharing in the joy and passion the child is experiencing.

BUILDING SELF-CONFIDENCE AND SELF-ESTEEM IN YOUNG CHILDREN ON THE SPECTRUM

Self-confidence and self-esteem are very strong protective factors for long-term well-being as well as being building blocks for resilience and independence. Self-confidence is a wonderful quality, although it may sometimes seem to be in short supply, especially for autistic people, even in those autistics who may appear to be overly confident. Self-confidence basically means you like and feel good about yourself and feel that you are good at what you do (work, study, relationships, interests and hobbies, etc.). When you are grounded and content, you will be less distressed by negative feedback and able to learn from failure.

Self-confidence and self-esteem need to be promoted and encouraged in all children and young people. Self-esteem can be seen when a person feels valued and worthwhile. All too frequently, autistic children experience discrimination, bullying and abuse. These sorts of things constitute invalidation. Invalidation is the enemy of self-confidence and self-esteem. Invalidation sends the message that someone is worthless and devalues them both to themselves and among their peers. It is very hard to be self-confident if you think – and are given ongoing messages – that you are worthless:

Joe does not communicate with speech; he can point to things or go and get things that he wants. However, at pre-school, the teachers are trying to support him to develop speech as his family have said that this is important to them. The way that the teachers do this is to keep asking Joe to 'use your words' when he points at or goes to get something. They will sometimes stop him from getting a toy or book and repeat their demand for him to use his words. After a few months, the other children at the pre-school started to treat Joe differently, responding to his presence by looking at him directly and saying, 'Use words Joe.' One of Joe's teachers asked for a family and team meeting to raise concerns about the messaging that Joe seemed to be getting as she had noticed his confidence was decreasing and he was interacting less and less.

Six months later, Joe was no longer being verbally prompted to use his words; instead, he had been taught how to use a simple visual communication system of pointing to photos of objects and activities. He was being asked to use this throughout the day to make choices about what he wanted or needed. The other children were also taught to use the choice board system, and it became a part of every group session, even when Joe was not part of the group. The other children stopped telling Joe to use his words and were instead observed going to collect a choice board and some photo cards when they wanted to find out if Joe wanted to play with them. Both the pre-school teachers and Joe's family noticed he appeared to be more confident and interactive with both adults and his peers.

Add autism into the mix and there is potentially a huge range of thoughts and messages about the child's perceived incompetence, deficits, failings and lack of value from all quarters – even their family and parents, at times. People who are supposed to be assisting the autistic child can, in fact, reinforce negative messages. This can be seen in Joe's story above where people who wanted to help Joe were assuming that speaking was a goal that would help him and that prompting him to speak was helpful. However, it was observed that their behaviour was sending Joe and his peers negative messages about Joe, which began to affect Joe and the way his peers treated him. Once this adult messaging changed, both Joe and his peers seemed to take on the new message that Joe was a capable communicator and that people *should* communicate with him in the way that was most meaningful to him.

It is very important to be aware of the messaging your child is receiving. While you can't really control what others say to them a lot of the time, keep a lookout for blaming or negative things said to – or about – your child from different places, including childcare, school, after school activities, and even clinicians and support workers. Many people don't realise the impact their negativity around autism has on children and their families. Your child does not need to be told they are a burden or be blamed for inciting bullying or invalidated in any other way:

As a teacher and autism consultant, I have worked with hundreds of children, families and teachers. It never ceases to amaze me what people will say about an autistic child in their hearing. However, about five years ago, I braved a conversation on this topic when I asked *why* the adults talked about the child within their hearing. It was very interesting to me, that the adults did not realise that the child *could* hear them, because they could not hear conversations from that far away. Many autistic children have exceptionally good hearing and unless adults understand this, they may think that they are being discreet, when they are not.

As a result, children have heard and taken on board the frustrations of families and educators as factual comments about themselves, even when these comments were not meant as factual comments, and certainly not meant to be overheard and taken on board by the autistic child. It is important to have open and frank conversations, but these must be respectful and solution-focused and, where they are not, they should *not* be held unless the child is not in the same room or in any space nearby. (Emma)

Attitudes around autism have a huge impact on autistic children's self-confidence and self-esteem. Try to keep messaging around your child and their autism positive where you can. There is a lot of literature around ideas like neurodiversity, where autism is described as a difference and not an inherent deficit. Autistic children raised with this attitude are likely to have a higher level of self-confidence and self-worth than those predominantly given messaging about their apparent deficiencies and failings. This is not to negate or dismiss the significant challenges autism can result in. Rather, it is to foster a view that your autistic child has value and worth as they are. The difficulties they experience may come from others' attitudes and actions too, and may not be attributable only to autism:

I was diagnosed in primary school, and I had a great specialist teacher who also had a diagnosis of Asperger's. She really helped me to understand that my brain may work differently to other people, but it still worked! She would tell me why I had to do things, not just to do them. Like capital letters, which I used to put in the middle of words, because that looked nice. She explained about how the grammar rules said sentences should start with a capital letter, and so should proper nouns, which are place names or the names of people. She explained that even though I liked the look, the teachers had to mark the writing down because the capitals were in the wrong place for the grammar rules, and that the teachers got distracted by these capital letters and so could not focus on the content of the writing. Other teachers had just told me it was wrong but not why, so I was starting to think that I was no good at writing, but now I know I am. (Luke)

Building self-confidence and self-esteem is a journey. Try to ensure that at each point of their journey, your child is being given a view of their strengths and what they can achieve. This will help them to be more resilient. It also has a great bonus too in that resiliently managing challenges and difficulties usually makes a child feel better about themselves and as such feeds into positive self-confidence and self-esteem.

IMPACTS OF RESILIENCE ON SCHOOLING AND SOCIAL INTERACTION

Resilience is a great quality for school children to have. It can mean that they have a higher level of self-confidence. They may be more able to challenge – and less likely to internalise any negative messaging targeted at them. They may be more confident to ask questions of the teacher, rather than sitting quietly not knowing what to do or using loud or volatile behaviour to avoid doing work that they do not understand.

In school settings, resilience can help your child value themselves as they are. A large issue for many autistic kids and teens is the idea that they need to 'belong' to a group in order to be accepted in the social structure of the school. Many of these groups are unhelpful, and often an autistic child is used and exploited by peers in a clique. A sense of self-worth backed up with some years of parents helping the child to build resilience can lessen the impact of the need to belong at whatever cost. Autistic children can also model resilience and self-confidence to their classmates.

Some autistic children can appear not to need or want friends, and parents and teachers need to find out if this is the case before trying to force them to make friends or interact with people more frequently. It is important to teach about what constitutes a friend and what is unkind or bad behaviour towards another person, so that children understand that not all people in the world are kind and trustworthy and that they can be protected by their parent, carer or teacher when others are unkind to them.

One issue that it is important to address is the idea of resilience as a counter to bullying. There is a terrible but sadly quite common statement that some educators tell parents – or worse still autistic children – that they will not be bullied if they 'get some resilience', or indeed that bullying is just a part of life and that they need to just deal with it. These statements are contrary to the message of this book. The issue here is that these statements around resilience are essentially victim-blaming and imply that it is the autistic child and his or her parent's responsibility to manage bullying.

Bullying is a whole-of-community issue and needs to be tackled on many levels, all of which are grounded in the idea that all people are of worth and valuable for being who they are.

In fact, being resilient actually is beneficial in tackling bullying, but that is not generally the meaning of these comments from educators. A child is about as likely to acquire resilience overnight in order to withstand cruel words or acts by bullies as they are to grow 16 inches taller overnight! In this instance, the perceived need for resilience is used to invalidate the experience of bullying and let the bully off the hook. If anyone tells your child to 'get some resilience' to address bullying, you have every right to challenge this and ask that the bullying behaviour be addressed.

CONTROLLED CHALLENGES AND SUPPORTED RISKS

Building and establishing a sense of resilience and independence can be seen to come from the child undertaking a set of controlled challenges – incrementally more challenging activities that build their strength and confidence to enable the child to get through difficulties and build resilience. These work for children of any age, teens and adults, and are effective with autistic and non-autistic people alike. The basis for encouraging resilience in your child starts with these controlled challenges.

This story is about an autistic adult, but illustrates the principle of controlled challenges:

Anna is 28 and has a diagnosis of autism spectrum condition and an anxiety disorder. Anna had a lot of stress around employment. She really wanted a job, but even thinking about applying for a job would make her extremely anxious. She was studying arts at university but worried she would never be able to work.

A friend suggested Anna do some volunteer work at the gallery she owned. Despite it being really stressful, Anna said yes as it was with a friend and it was volunteer work, so she thought the level of expectation around her performance would not be so daunting. Initially, Anna only worked one shift a week at the gallery. Her job was mostly publicity – sending out invitations and managing the gallery's email traffic. Anna's friend told her she was a great volunteer employee. Anna was surprised and happy. She found she actually liked working once she got used to doing all the things she needed to do. Her friend asked her if she would like to do two shifts a week. Anna did this and it went really well. Anna still didn't feel ready for paid work with an employer she didn't know, but she wanted to challenge herself a bit more. She started a small business, designing websites as she enjoyed coding. This work was great because Anna could decide the hours and how many jobs she took on. After about six months, the manager of an online retailer contacted Anna and said that she had seen her websites and thought they were great. She offered Anna a paid position in the business. Even though a couple of years previously Anna would have been completely unable to consider this work, she was now much more confident and accepted the job, She is still working there and also has some other clients.

The sorts of controlled challenges you start giving your child at an early age can result in the child being independent, more willing to take on new things and manage change when they mature. If we go back to the Introduction of this book, Adam was a child who had been shielded from difficulties throughout childhood. The impact this had on him was twofold – he was extremely anxious around anything going wrong and he was unable to do the things that most young adults can do like study, employment or living independently. Of course, you need to get the balance right as you don't want the challenge to become traumatic or increase your child's stress levels to a point that the exercise backfires and they end up more anxious about the change than before. It is important to note that a child's ability to take on something new will change depending on a number of factors and will be different each day. Be aware of anything that might have made your child more – or less – vulnerable in recent days and hours. As the parent, you will be the best judge of how your child is progressing with each controlled challenge. You will need to observe their response to the challenge and how they feel about it. You do not need to adhere strictly to a schedule around controlled challenges. There is no harm in postponing or cancelling a particular challenge if it is too much and may be more harmful than beneficial.

The challenges should be manageable and not the sorts of things that cause trauma. However, it is important to come from the view that you are challenging your child and they may not be entirely happy about this. A problem that can occur is when parents worry too much about upsetting their child or they want to be their child's best friend. A parent of adult children can be their friend, but parents of young children would be better placed to see their role as a facilitator or a supportive and beneficial manager. Your child needs you – with your experience, wisdom and understanding – to guide them through their life and to set limits when required.

Autistic children particularly need this guidance. If you want to see yourself as your child's friend, that is fine, but the relationship between a child and his or her parents is a different dynamic to a friendship. You are doing your child a favour by challenging them and if they don't immediately love you for it, that is okay. In addition, the role of a teacher is to challenge as well as nurture, but if school is the first place that a child encounters challenge, it can be overwhelming for them. This is another reason to challenge young children, to help prepare them for the challenges they will need to manage in pre-school and school.

This book will provide information around expectations and appropriate challenges at different life stages and milestones for autistic children. The activities can be done in any order, or you may find it more useful to start at the beginning and work through them sequentially. You may already have done some things that are similar to some of the activities, in which case your child will benefit from having their learning reinforced.

CHAPTER 2

COMMON CHARACTERISTICS OF AUTISTIC CHILDREN BETWEEN AGES TWO AND SEVEN

EARLY CHILDHOOD DIAGNOSIS

In recent years, more very young children from 18 months old have been gaining autism diagnoses. The diagnosis should be a valuable attribute that enables people to understand the child and therefore provide effective support for that child. Some parents – and friends of parents or extended family members – don't think a child should be 'labelled'. This is often an unhelpful attitude. The autism diagnosis has two main functions: the first is that it opens the door to appropriate services and support. Without the 'label', most services cannot be accessed or need to be funded fully by the parent. With the diagnosis, children can have access to support services and useful things like learning support units at school, speech therapy and occupational therapy.

The other main function of a diagnostic label is also incredibly important: that is, the idea of autistic identity. Autistic people tend to share some characteristics with other people who are on the autism spectrum. Put an autistic person in a room full of other autistic people and they will almost certainly be more comfortable than if they were in a room full of non-autistic strangers. Autism can be seen as a different culture. Without the label, that culture is harder to access. This is the case for autistic people from cradle to grave – autism is an integral part of who they are. While a 3-year-old is probably not going to consciously identify as autistic in the way an adult or teen might, parents can introduce them to autistic peers and role models throughout their childhood and teen years. The diagnostic label is the door to autistic culture and that culture can make the difference between a child who feels supported, included and understood, and one who is socially isolated. Access to autistic culture can boost self-confidence and feelings of self-worth, in the same way that access to Deaf culture is important for deaf people.

Some people seem to think that seeking a 'label' for a child through a diagnosis will somehow make them more autistic or result in an inappropriate or unnecessary diagnosis. This is unlikely. A competent diagnostician will not give a child a diagnosis if they don't qualify for one. It is worth being aware that some diagnosticians are less thorough than others and there is a potential for a conflict of interest if further funding may be directed towards that person if and only if they diagnose autism. Children with other sensory, physical or cognitive difficulties or delays should be seen by specialist paediatric teams, who may prefer to wait until the child is older before making a definitive diagnosis. Other conditions, such as hearing loss, can result in behaviours that are similar to behaviours that are observed in autistic children and vice versa.

The diagnosis should be a description or acknowledgement of characteristics that exist in the child already. It is a bit like an explorer finding a waterfall. The waterfall was always there. It didn't magically come into existence just because someone who didn't know it was there came across it! Try to see the diagnostic label as you and your child's friend, opening doors to services that will help them navigate life successfully and also give them membership to their own 'club' filled with people who share similar experiences and understandings of the wider world.

An early or very early diagnosis can be an amazing gift. You will be able to better understand your child and access helpful services for them from a young age. Many autistic people diagnosed in adulthood or teenage years wish they had a diagnosis as a small child as they feel it would have helped them understand themselves better and to navigate the school environment better. This is not to say that early intervention is vital for an autistic child to achieve their potential, nor to endorse intensive early intervention, which can be detrimental to young children trying to learn to be comfortable with who they are.

TELLING YOUNG CHILDREN ABOUT THEIR DIAGNOSIS

A very common question posed to autistic conference speakers by large numbers of parents is when is it the right time to tell their child about their diagnosis. Autism is likely to be a very important factor in your child's development through life. It is not anything to hide or be ashamed of, so it makes sense to tell the child – in whatever way parents choose – as soon as they get the diagnosis. This situation can be seen as being similar to when a child is adopted in a closed adoption arrangement. Some parents will keep their adoption from the child. In films on the topic, there is always the scene where the child finds the adoption papers and is devastated. You don't want to make the autism diagnosis like the child finding their adoption papers. Tell them in whatever way works for you and them and then help use that diagnosis and what it comes with to build their sense of identity and self-knowledge as they grow to adulthood. Jackson's story may give some of the sense of normality that he has about his diagnosis; autism to him is just a part of who he is – no more stigmatising or problematic than wearing glasses.

JACKSON'S STORY

When I started school, I told my teacher I was autistic, and she smiled at me. She asked me about Thomas the Tank Engine. I love Thomas. No-one else in my class was autistic, but we had a girl who wears glasses and a boy with a hearing aid. We all learn a bit differently: the girl could not learn without her glasses, and I can't learn if there is too much noise, just like the boy with the hearing aid.

With very young children, it can be hard to know just how you are going to go about explaining their autism to them. In Australia, there is an organisation called Yellow Ladybugs, which provides social groups for young girls on the autism spectrum from about ages 5 and up. The girls are never told they are autistic by group organisers, but they are called 'yellow ladybugs'. This is a way of explaining difference and autistic identity in a way the girls can relate to, and which enables parents to acknowledge their daughters' identity without the need to talk about autism specifically.

Another group in Australia, I CAN, runs peer mentoring sessions for neurodiverse children, which are called 'imagination clubs', where children are given tips from autistic adults using their lived experience. Other groups, such as Asperlutely Autsome or regional/national autism groups, are more explicit about the child's diagnosis. There are some great resources for talking about autism to young children, including Kathy Hoopman's book *All Cats Have Asperger Syndrome* (2006, Jessica Kingsley Publishers). It is important to let children know that a range of adults are autistic, so that they understand that the diagnosis does not limit their life in any way; rather, that it is a tool to help them manage their life in the most effective way.

Children react differently to being told about their autism. For some, it is matter of fact and just another piece of information, and for others it can be challenging and even traumatic, especially if the news is delivered in any kind of negative way. Very young children tend not to have a clear and cohesive sense of identity, so when introducing the discussion around their autism, it will probably be best to come from the position of just introducing the idea, much in the same way you describe their relationship to their siblings and cousins, or the fact that they have brown or black hair or particular colour eyes. It is something they need to know about themselves. As they get older, you can introduce more information about autism and what it means. Many children will start to ask questions about their autism as they grow older, whether or not the parent has told them. This is because autistics usually feel quite different to the majority of their peers, and they want to know why they do not understand others and others do not understand them. With very young children, the notion of them being on the autism spectrum can be incorporated into their understanding of themselves and their position in the world from so early in their life that they won't remember a time when they didn't know about that piece of all the things that make them who they are. This can impact positively on their sense of self.

EXPLAINING THE PROCESS OF ASSESSMENT TO CHILDREN

Young children are unlikely to understand concepts around the process and implications of an assessment for autism. The process might be confusing or frightening. As with any new activity, autistic children will respond better to a diagnostic assessment if they are forewarned about what is likely to happen.

Preparing young children for events that might be overwhelming, confusing or unpredictable is a really important part of raising autistic children. New situations and unpredictable change can result in overload and meltdown or shutdown. This can be prevented, and it is one of the important things that parents can do to help autistic children: teach them to manage change.

The notion of resilience has at its core the idea of facing new and challenging situations, and building confidence and mastery. If you can help your child develop their skill even before they are assessed for autism, you are doing an excellent job. A lot of this comes down to understanding your child and the issues and triggers they experience around change and how to support them to come through the change well.

Things like Social Stories™ or comic strips can be helpful when undertaking something as challenging as the explanation of an autism assessment. It is important to use the ways to communicate that are the most meaningful and engaging for your child. For example, you could talk about what might happen through telling a story or drawing pictures using your child's favourite character, such as My Little Pony or Pokémon or a particular animal. You can also use toys to model or demonstrate what can happen, as long as you use very clear and explicit language. Please refer to the Useful Resources section of this book for further information on Social Stories™.

TALKING TO SCHOOL/CHILDCARE ABOUT DIAGNOSIS

Some parents do not want to disclose their child's diagnosis to childcare or school, for a variety of reasons, mainly around not wanting people to place limitations on the expectations for their child. However, it is usually a good idea to disclose to relevant people in your child's 'world', including their school and/or childcare centre, so that they can understand your child and plan appropriate and effective supports. Knowing exactly whom to tell can be difficult though. As a general rule, telling your child's classroom teacher/s, the school principal and staff who look after your child at childcare is a good idea. If the child's diagnosis is kept hidden from these people, then you will not be able to access any supports or interventions at the school. Bear in mind that most countries protect your child's rights to education if they have a diagnosis; where this is not the case, you may want to discuss options with your local autism association or support group.

In addition, your child may be unfairly treated if educators do not know about their autism diagnosis. The pre-school teacher may assume that your child is a poorly behaved child instead of realising that they are an autistic child who may be struggling to manage what can be a sensorially overwhelming environment. A disclosed diagnosis actually opens the door to services and supports that can help enable your child to succeed at school. That being said, there can be issues with educators not understanding autism or being judgemental, but generally disclosure to relevant adults involved in your child's education and care is a good idea. It is useful to explain what the diagnosis means for *your* child, rather than simply stating the diagnosis. For example, you may want to share some or all of the diagnostic report, or a summary of their current strengths and difficulties.

There is also the issue of whether or not to disclose to other parents from your child's school or childcare. This can be more difficult than the decision around disclosing to educators. Educators are more likely to have some knowledge of autism and will almost certainly have worked with autistic children before. Other parents tend to be less predictable and consistent in terms of their responses. If your child has some behaviours that may be perceived as unusual – and particularly if they can be viewed as being aggressive to other children – other parents may well be judgemental and think your child is 'bad' or comes from a neglectful or abusive family. In this situation, disclosing can be helpful as it allows other parents to understand that there is a legitimate reason for your child acting in a way that is not typical.

However, many parents do not know a lot about autism. Even if you disclose to them, the diagnosis alone may not enable them to understand why your child is behaving in an unexpected way. One thing that autism parents and autistic people often do is to approach the conversation around autism with some assumed knowledge. They might say 'my child is autistic' and expect the other person to have a similar level of knowledge and understanding of autism as they do, when in fact the other person has very little idea of what autism means. Therefore, when disclosing your child's autism to anyone – parent, teacher, etc. – it will help to explain what autism is and, most importantly, what it means for your child.

CHAPTER 3

WHAT ARE SOME COMMON CHALLENGES FOR YOUNG CHILDREN ON THE AUTISM SPECTRUM?

Young children on the autism spectrum can experience a number of challenges around navigating the world. These include not having a diagnosis. An appropriate diagnosis can make all the difference for an autistic child. Without the diagnosis, their behaviour might be seen as being inappropriate, aggressive or disruptive, particularly in school or childcare settings. The child may miss out on services that can assist their development, such as speech therapy or occupational therapy. Not all children require these services, but when they do, they can have a bigger impact more quickly when provided earlier in life. Because of differences in the male and female presentation of autism,[1] which will be discussed later in this chapter, girls might be diagnosed later than boys, and some girls struggle to get a diagnosis at all.

Other adults may judge the child as being disobedient or a 'bad influence' and tell their own children to keep away. This can put the autistic child at a social disadvantage from a very early age, and this may be a 'label' that follows them throughout their school years, resulting in social isolation and dislocation:

HARRY'S STORY (TOLD BY HIS MUM, WITH HARRY'S CONSENT)

Harry did not get a diagnosis until he was an adult; he really struggled at kindergarten and school. His behaviour was quite difficult as he would have large numbers of very physical meltdowns, which meant

---

1 This refers to general differences. Individual girls and boys with autism may be closer to the more typically female or male presentation of autism.

the other children were frightened of him and the teachers got fed up with him very quickly. As a family, we had no idea what was causing his outbursts and thought all kinds of things. I am really sad that Harry really did not get any kind of proper understanding or support until he was an adult, when ultimately he needed very little support. If, as a child, his sensory needs and anxiety had been managed, we think he would have done so much better at school and in turn not been so socially isolated.

As well as enabling parents to access appropriate and timely support for their child, a diagnosis means that parents can have conversations around autism with significant people in their child's life (such as childcare workers, teachers and other family members). It also enables parents to participate in social and support groups for parents of autistic kids and for the child to participate in programs for autistic or neurodiverse children. This connection to community – both for the child and his/her parents – can be a strong support and a protective factor.

COMMUNICATION DIFFERENCES

Autistic communication is generally quite different from non-autistic communication, whether or not speech is used. Historically, autistic communication has been seen as deficient or ineffective, and to a large extent it is still thought of in this way. Things like eye contact and body language are seen as being essential for 'proper' communication, at least in the Western, English-speaking world. This can result in children being forced to make eye contact or constantly told to do something or other differently with their body or posture.

These sorts of interventions, instead of helping the child, can, in fact, result in them being more anxious in social settings as they try to remember and implement all the things they have been told to do. Research has found that autistic children forced to behave in ways that are unnatural for them are negatively impacted across a range of developmental objectives, including spoken language. Eye contact in particular can be very difficult and unpleasant for many autistic people, both children and adults. It can feel like the person is being invaded or physically assaulted, or be experienced as an incredibly intense interaction with another person, rendering it impossible for them to actually hear what the speaker is saying to them. However, many of these apparent 'essentials' for communication are, in fact, not essential at all.

It is a good idea to view autistic and non-autistic communication styles like two different languages. For example, imagine autistic communication is French and non-autistic communication is Chinese. When a roomful of French people are speaking, they all understand one another. Similarly, when a roomful of Chinese people are speaking Mandarin, they understand one another. But what happens when a French speaker goes into a roomful of Chinese people and tries to communicate? They cannot make themselves understood, despite being completely capable of communicating in their own language. Likewise, a group of autistic people will usually understand one another's communication style, but placed in a situation where all the communication is in the non-autistic style, they are often at a loss and may seem inept at communication. Just as you wouldn't say French is deficient because it isn't Mandarin, autistic communication can be viewed as a valid other 'language' or culture. The good news is that just as Mandarin speakers can learn French, so too can non-autistic people 'learn' autistic communication. It does not need to go all in the one direction of trying to teach autistic children to be more non-autistic – parents and carers can learn 'autistic' communication too and meet their children halfway! In fact, it would seem obvious that it is better for people to meet halfway, rather than to expect autistic children to abandon their natural way of communicating and learn a whole new way, when one of the diagnostic criteria for the autism spectrum is a difficulty with social communication.

SOCIAL ISSUES AT SCHOOL/CHILDCARE

Autistic children can often come up against social or behavioural issues at school, childcare or pre-school. These can be in response to overload and meltdowns or for a number of other reasons. The term 'social issues' can, unfortunately, also be used to describe victimisation of an autistic child by bullies, as if the autistic child is somehow deliberately provoking the bullies. One thing to be aware of with autistic children and bullying is that often bullying is quite 'one-sided'. The autistic child is not trying to provoke the bully but their very existence and appearance of 'difference' results in bullies attacking them. However, in rare instances, autistic children themselves can participate in bullying behaviour – either as a 'genuine' bully or in order to be accepted by peers and avoid being victimised themselves. This needs addressing as would any other bullying behaviour.

Some young autistic children can be aggressive towards other children, and this can often be misinterpreted as bullying. Some things that may result in aggression in autistic children include:

- meltdowns due to sensory, social and/or emotional overload

- copying of, or retaliation against, violence or teasing from another child

- feeling personal space is being invaded by other children and lacking the means to communicate this to the child through verbal or 'peaceful' means

- perceived threat of aggression from other children, whether real or imagined

- as a misunderstood part of play or games.

The first two of the above points can be understood as instinctive survival behaviour, as the child tries to fight or run away.

Some autistic children may have well-developed imaginative play but may be quite controlling. So, while they think up a game or role play, they might stage-manage the other children to ensure the game is 'correct': autistic children can find other children not following the rules of their game distressing. Other children may not want to play with the autistic child because they feel bossed around or controlled. In a similar vein, some autistic children are very focused on rules and are concerned if they think one of their peers is breaking a rule. While they are correct that the school has rules, being the 'rules police' can lead to a child being unpopular with their peers.

ANXIETY

Anxiety is unfortunately almost a constant companion for many autistic people, both children and adults; although they may or may not know that they are experiencing anxiety, their bodies will respond to the chemical triggers in their brains that are set off by anxiety. This instinctive response can result in what is often described as a 'meltdown', but is in fact just the human survival instincts of fight, flight or freeze/hide.

Children can be extremely anxious or worried about a range of activities and experiences. New activities, people or places can result in severe anxiety. Anxiety is the enemy of resilience in some respects as it hinders a child from taking on new challenges or situations. Anxiety should be understood and respected but also gently challenged to ensure children do not become too sheltered. If everything that causes your child anxiety is removed, it will be almost impossible for them to take on new challenges and resilience. This can be a very delicate balance and should be frequently revised. There will be further information on addressing and working with anxiety in the specific activities later in this book.

FRUSTRATION

Autistic children can become very frustrated with a range of activities including, but not limited to: playing by themselves, interacting with others and their schoolwork. Autistic children often struggle with the concept of 'practice makes perfect'. When being taught a new skill, they can become very frustrated and angry, particularly if they make a mistake or do not understand what they are meant to be doing. Autistic children are also more likely than their neurotypical peers to be perfectionists, even at a very young age. Perfectionism can result in a sort of activity paralysis or anxiety around a subject or activity that they may even have previously enjoyed.

It is important to note that some of the experiences autistic children encounter may not be related to their autism but to the mismatch that can occur when they find themselves in the largely non-autistic world. Non-autistic adults can help bridge this gap through understanding autism and the child's character. This does not just need to be the child's parents but also pre-school and primary school teachers, health professionals and other family members. Adults are in a much better position to understand and support autistic children than the children are to figure out the nuances and complexities of the 'other language' that is non-autistic communication. Thus, when autistic children reply honestly to a rhetorical question, it is important that the child *not* be told off; rather, the questioner should realise that the autistic child rarely, if ever, understands that social context and the appropriate reply to a rhetorical question is completely different to the context and response to a genuine question.

General characteristics of the autism spectrum

These characteristics are often shared by all children/adults on the autism spectrum, and include:

- difficulties interacting with the non-autistic world

- passionate interests in a topic

- very 'one-level' way of communicating – autistic people do not tend to use manipulation, sarcasm or anything that relies on what is being said not tallying with what the autistic person understands is true

- trusting and naïve – while a good quality in general, this can also result in abuse by predatory people

- subject to victimisation, bullying, violence and abuse – this is not the 'fault' of the autistic child or autism generally, it is a symptom of a lack of respect and understanding around perceived 'difference'

- different/heightened sensory experiences that can be so intense as to cause physical pain or overload

- high level of anxiety

- difficulties dealing with change and new situations.

There are some qualities that autistic people have that are as individual as for non-autistic people:

- *Intellect.* Despite the 'genius' stereotype, autistic people have the same range of cognitive ability and intellect as the general population.

- *Sexuality.* Some people believe that autistic people are all asexual. This is not true. While a percentage of autistic people are asexual, many have sexual relationships and have children, and the full spectrum of sexualities and gender identities is represented.

- *Sense of humour.* Autistic people come with the full range of types of sense of humour. The stereotype that they don't understand jokes is the case for some, but many autistic people love to laugh, and to make other people laugh. There are a lot of autistic comedians.

- *Technology.* Not all autistic people are good at using technology or have an affinity with it.

It is also important to understand that autistic people – like all people – are all individuals. A lot of elements of your autistic child's personality and character are them being who they are. You do not need to pathologise or label every action and thought an autistic child has. It does tend to happen that when parents or others get a diagnosis for a child, everything their child experiences is seen through the lens of autism.

Autistic people have a greater incidence of divergent gender and gender identity differences than the non-autistic population. Differences in identities – for example, identifying as transgender – can occur at quite young ages and impact on the gendered presentation of autism. The value of understanding these gendered differences in autism is that you can have a heads-up about difficulties your child may be having and present your observations to a diagnostician who may be reluctant to give an autism diagnosis.

PROTECTIVE FACTORS AND RISK FACTORS FOR YOUNG AUTISTIC CHILDREN

As with the acquisition of any skill, resilience can be helped or hindered by a range of things. These can be seen as risk and protective factors. Focusing on promoting and building protective factors is an essential step in the process of promoting resilience in your autistic child. Conversely, addressing and decreasing or avoiding risk factors can ease your child's journey to resilience and independence.

A key protective factor for resilience in young children on the autism spectrum is the ability to communicate effectively with peers and adults. Communication is a skill learnt throughout a person's life, but for autistic kids it is particularly critical. Communication does not necessarily just mean speech. Many autistic children are non-verbal or take longer to start to speak than their typical peers. The reason effective communication is such a key factor is that autistic children need to make sense of their world and convey their concerns and thoughts to the adults in their life. They need to understand all the unexpected and unpredictable things that happen in life. A parent or sibling who understands their communication and can communicate – information, explanations and so on – back to the child, will make that child's life considerably less stressful.

There is a lot of confusion around non-verbal autistic children, with some people presuming that a lack of verbal speech indicates intellectual disability or demonstrates that the person has nothing to say. While some autistic children – including some who are non-verbal – do have an intellectual disability in addition to their autism, many non-verbal autistic people have similar or above average intellect and cognitive ability. They may have a lot to say, but lack the ability to say it verbally, or the understanding that the spoken word is a form of communication.

The focus for non-verbal autistic children should not simply be to get them to speak. One of the biggest issues for a non-verbal person is effective communication, so, if they can't speak, then make something that works for them right now. If parents wait until the child speaks – which they may never do – all the time spent waiting for them to speak will be time they are stressed and extremely frustrated, wanting to communicate but not having the available means. All communication strategies support the development of speech, where this will happen; they do not hinder the development of speech. This includes sign, pictures and technology communication systems.

Another key factor in developing an autistic child's resilience is a supportive school/childcare environment. An autistic child's progress can be derailed if they go to a school or childcare centre that does not validate them and support their needs. It is important for staff and teachers working with your child to understand their needs and their personality. For parents of autistic children, there is often more contact with educators and support staff than for parents of typical students. Doing what you can to ensure the childcare centre or school is an environment where your child is accepted and supported is really important. This means that you all need to work collaboratively, understanding one another's roles and stressors, seeking solutions rather than blame. This can be difficult when the child behaves quite differently in one environment compared to another, which is usual for autistic children.

Often, childcare or school is the first place that children come into contact with large groups of other children. If the transition from the home environment to childcare or school environment is a largely positive one that allows the child to take on social and other challenges in a supportive environment, this can set up your child for a more positive experience of schooling. This in turn will allow them to build resilience as they journey through education. There are practical activities and further information on beginning school and childcare later in this book.

Being exposed to challenges and overcoming them is the basis of all resilience – the notion of taking on a challenge and coming out the other side of it with more mastery of that challenge and more confidence. For autistic children – and everyone – there is often a fine line between taking on too much challenge and failing and taking on challenges appropriate to the individual, which allow them to succeed. The activities and information in this book will help you to get that balance right. However, it is important to trust your judgement as parents, too. You know your child better than the authors of this book ever will. If you view the activities and strategies in this book through the lens of your own understanding of your child, you will probably gain the best results.

Social support and friends are key aspects to being resilient in terms of mental health and well-being. Having genuine friends and social contact can be a strong protective factor for resilience. It is an area to focus attention on. Genuine friends do not need to be other autistic kids, although they often are. Other neurodiverse children, such as those with dyslexia and/or dyspraxia, are also often more easily able to instinctively understand and relate positively to autistic children, as are highly empathic children and young people. Social contacts with extended or immediate family can also form a strong protective factor.

When thinking about friendships, it can be helpful to keep in mind that being comfortable in yourself around other people is the most important aspect of a friendship for many autistics. This means that playing alongside or sharing time together with an activity of interest may be more meaningful in terms of social support than more typical friend-type activities of standing around talking or playing group games.

NAVIGATING AVAILABLE SERVICES

It is important to know what is available: there will be free/funded and private services available in most areas. Autism services are not 'good' just because they are free or they cost a lot of money. It is important to evaluate not only what is available, but whether or not the service will support your child to develop their potential without causing any unintended harm. Looking at the research evidence for different types of support services and strategies is very important. Anything that says it will cure your child is unlikely to be of any benefit as there is no cure for autism, nor is there a need for a cure. Also, anything that requires long-term commitment in terms of time and/or money needs to be carefully evaluated – is there an alternative that is more doable for you and your child, which allows your child to have time to be a child rather than constantly attending intervention/support services/therapies.

Andrew Whitehouse, Winthrop Professor at the Telethon Kids Institute, University of Western Australia, has written extensively about how to choose support services for your autistic child. He recommends that you ask the provider the following questions:

- *What is the therapy?* You need to know what this therapy actually involves.

- *What is the rationale of the therapy?* You need to know why this therapy may be effective for your child.

- *Is the therapy safe?* You need to know that this therapy will not harm your child.

- *Is the therapy effective?* You need to know if there is scientific evidence that this therapy can lead to improvements.[2]

---

2   Whitehouse, A. (2016) *A Guide for How to Choose Therapy for a Child with Autism*. Available at: http://theconversation.com/a-guide-for-how-to-choose-therapy-for-a-child-with-autism-64729 (accessed 28 June 2017).

TYPES OF SUPPORT OR RESOURCE

- *Assessment.* Depending on where you live, different types of assessment or providers will be required to complete the assessment for you or your child to access funding for supports, whether these are for education or communication, and so on. Check with your paediatrician, GP or local autism organisation for relevant and up-to-date information around assessment processes and procedures.

- *Psychologists.* Can offer support services to promote well-being and resilience. These are usually most effective if the psychologist has a good understanding of the autism spectrum and is comfortable and skilled at communicating in an autistic-friendly manner.

- *Psychiatrists.* As for psychologists, although psychiatrists can also prescribe psychiatric medications if these would be beneficial. This applies to a very small number of autistic children and young people. However, management of anxiety and/or depression can be more effective with psychiatric supports in place.[3]

- *Public health services,* including **mental health services**. May offer a range of support services for autistic children, young people, adults and/or their families.

- *Books and blogs around many aspects of autism exist.* When reading these, it is important to ask if they are accurate and useful or not. For example, when a blog is focusing on curing autism, the supports suggested are not likely to be helpful or effective.

- *Support groups – online and face-to-face – for parents and kids.* These can also vary in quality and interaction style. Parent-run groups tend to have a different tone and focus to autistic adult-run groups (some are run by autistic adults who are parents to autistic children). Autistic adult-run groups tend to use autistic communication styles, which are honest and to the point, but that can be confronting for people who are not expecting this.

---

3   Purkis J., Goodall, E. and Nugent, J. (2016) *The Guide to Good Mental Health on the Autism Spectrum.* London: Jessica Kingsley Publishers.

- *Respite services.* To qualify for respite services, whether these are paid for or funded by your regional/national government, your child and family circumstances usually need to have been assessed by either psychiatric and/or social work professionals. There are daytime, brief, overnight and longer-term respite services in many countries. Autism-specific respite services are often oversubscribed with very long waiting lists and it may be that your child will receive as good a service from a non-autism-specific service, depending on their needs, age, interests and so on.

- *Making connections.* Having these with other parents to share what works well along the journey of raising your child can be a great support. It is important to note that these connections are not always useful or helpful, especially if the other parents are stuck in a negative mindset. However, if you can offer one another mutual support, by, for example, having a babysitting circle, this can make a huge positive impact on all the families. Some pre-schools, childcare centres and/or schools have already got parent groups for parents of children with additional needs. If your child's centre or school does not, you could ask for assistance to set one up.

AUTISTIC PEER GROUP/PEER MENTORING

Even for young children on the spectrum, connecting with other autistic children and adults is very beneficial for their mental health and sense of identity and self-worth. If you ask any autistic adult about how they felt when meeting other autistic adults, most will tell you how valuable and meaningful the experience was of meeting others who are 'like them'. In non-autistic society, autistic people are often left on the periphery, being ostracised, excluded or just lacking the confidence to break into conversations and interact with their typical peers.

There is an increasing number of programs in many cities where autistic children can get together for social outings or shared activities with other autistic children. One example of this is the Spectrum Playgroup in New Zealand. This is a very successful model of a playgroup for young children on the autism spectrum. Parents are involved and children do a range of activities. For some on the spectrum, meeting autistic peers is easier and can help to develop a strong sense of belonging. Even if there isn't a group in your local area, meeting up with other families with autistic children can help your child to find their own autistic peer group.

If there are no groups like this in your area, you could set up a group modelled on an existing group from somewhere else. You may even be able to access a grant to help you with set-up costs, such as hall rental or advertising.

Another group in Australia, Asperlutely Autsome, run groups not just for autistic children, but their siblings and the whole family. They have camps, Lego clubs, computer groups, and so on. If you live elsewhere, you could set up a group modelled on an existing group from somewhere else.

WHAT DOES RESILIENCE LOOK LIKE IN A YOUNG CHILD ON THE AUTISM SPECTRUM?

It is sometimes hard to quantify how changes have happened for a young child who is being assisted to build his or her resilience. Changes may be subtle and not immediately obvious.

Young children on the autism spectrum who have gained some resilience are more likely to be:

- more self-confident

- more able to take on new challenges

- able to ask for help when needed

- less frightened of change or new situations

- less aggressive or difficult when around other people

- more able to set and respond to boundaries.

These resilient toddlers and young children will be more willing to engage with a range of experiences in life, including experimenting with activities, foods and clothing, and interacting with new and less familiar people. They will be less upset for less time than non-resilient toddlers and young children and more able and willing to learn from mistakes and manage disappointment and change.

CHAPTER 4

LIFE EVENTS FOR YOUNG AUTISTIC CHILDREN

Strategies and Activities around Building Resilience

This chapter will focus on a number of life events and developmental milestones that autistic children aged 2–6 years old are likely to experience. It will include a description of the life event and what specific issues it might pose for autistic children. Each milestone will also include information on what a good outcome might look like, as well as activities and strategies parents can put in place to help their child develop resilience and set the foundations for independence through navigating through that life event.

TRYING NEW FOODS

Many – but not all – autistic children and even adults can experience a variety of difficulties with food and eating. For young autistic children, one of the most challenging issues around food can be trying new foods. Many autistic children will only eat food with a similar taste, texture, colour or appearance. It is often hard to establish a balanced diet. Some autistic children will only eat a tiny range of foods, and introducing new foods can be very difficult. Some young autistic children can become fixated on eating foods that are only hard (or soft) and brown (or white), so the introduction of new foods needs to start quite young to ensure that autistic children are able to access a balanced and varied diet throughout life. Food refusal for autistic children is not usually a choice, or being fussy. It is more a case of 'can't eat' than 'won't eat'.

Unfortunately, mealtimes can become a bit of a battleground in some families, with parents desperate for their children to try one new food or eat more than the few things they eat, which may not be nutritionally balanced. This will not build resilience and can result in long-term issues around food and mealtimes for the children. It is also worth bearing in mind that for some autistic children, context can impact food choices and willingness to try new things significantly. So, for example, a child who is usually comfortable and relaxed around mealtimes and food may not be during things like birthday parties or school/pre-school events. Even visiting friends and relatives can result in significant anxiety around foods for some autistic children. Conversely, many teachers report that a significant number of autistic children with strong food preferences are willing to try new foods at school camps or during cooking/food and nutrition classes.

A variety of things can result in limited eating and rejecting new foods. Humans are programmed to try and avoid dangerous foods by spitting out or vomiting foods that are perceived as poisonous. Often in nature, bright colours signify that a plant or insect is toxic to those planning to eat it. Only when there is familiarity with the colour, smell, texture and taste of a particular food will anyone be completely comfortable eating that food. As an example, some people are really happy eating cheese that smells like smelly socks, because they know that it does not taste like it smells. However, without being confident in that knowledge, people may take tiny bites or experiment with touching the food with their lips and/or nose first.

Eating is a very sensory-stimulating experience. It involves the sense of taste of course, but also smell and touch and interoception, which signal thirst, hunger and satiety. Eating can involve a sensory onslaught, which can be very hard for children to articulate or for parents to explain. Pushing the food away or spitting it out may not be intentional poor manners/rudeness, and these strategies are useful when food is off or tastes otherwise dangerous to the child. The child may be completely overwhelmed by the combination of sensory experiences and respond in the only way they think they can by expelling the cause of the overload.

As some autistic people have heightened sensory awareness, an unpleasant taste or smell may be magnified. If foods have caused difficulties and overload in the past, the child may be highly anxious every time they are asked to try a new or unrecognised food. This can result in heightened anxiety around eating and mealtimes. In households where parents force children to try a new food or to finish everything on their plate, this anxiety often becomes immense and can lead to eating disorders in the long term. However, when children see adults eating a variety of food and trying small amounts of new foods from time to time, they are more likely to be willing to try these new foods, too.

Be careful around hiding vegetables in other dishes. Autistic children often have heightened senses, including smell and taste. So, while a non-autistic child might not be aware of the finely grated zucchini in their pasta, an autistic child might not only spot the offending vegetable but also lose trust in the person who served them the food – usually a parent. The child will think they have been tricked, and this loss of trust can impact a range of other areas beyond mealtimes:

> I was a very fussy eater as a child, but my mum worked out quite quickly that I was willing to eat a much larger variety of foods if I only had a small amount of food on my plate, preferably no more than one of everything. So, one pea, one piece of carrot, one piece of potato, etc. If there was more than one, I would get overwhelmed and refuse to eat. Mum always made me try one bite of something new as she said, 'You can't know if you will or won't like something unless you try it.' Now, as an adult, I am quite adventurous with what I will eat. (Amy)

Despite all these barriers to eating a balanced diet, parents rightly want their children to eat a range of foods. Starting a healthy diet early in life is often a good indicator for healthy eating habits in adulthood. It is therefore important to introduce new foods to autistic children, but it needs to be done in a way that supports the child and does not result in unintended consequences such as the child being even more anxious around food and mealtimes. Nederkoorn et al. (2015) found that children with tactile sensitivities (those who struggle to touch a variety of textures comfortably) are more fussy eaters as the texture of foods in their mouth can be problematic for them:

> I hate having wet sticky things touching my fingers or hands; as a child the idea of finger painting was horrendous. Yuck! I also hated the wet slimy texture of some foods, like tofu or lychee. So disgusting, it really made my whole body feel yucky. Hard crunchy dry food was nice, but slimy stuff, urgh, I still can't eat it! (Lincoln)

Some parents use vitamins and diet supplements as an interim measure to ensure their child gets enough nutrition. While your child eating a balanced diet is the ideal, it can take a while to get them into a pattern of heathy eating. In this instance, dietary supplements and vitamins can be helpful.

PREFERRED OUTCOMES: A CHILD WHO IS RELAXED AND CONFIDENT AROUND FOOD

Anxiety around food can be purely a response to sensory issues and/or it can be a form of anxiety about change, so the sorts of supports designed to build confidence and resilience around change should also assist with some food issues. Some autistic children will struggle with food right up until and during adulthood.

Some signs that your child is doing well with their diet include:

- They can express their anxiety around trying a new food.

- Their anxiety around new food can be de-escalated.

- Your child can consider trying a new food without significant anxiety.

- If your child tries a new food and dislikes it strongly, it does not stop them from trying another different food at a later date.

- They are less distressed or not stressed around going to a different house or place where different food is served (e.g. a child's birthday party or a relative's house).

ACTIVITIES AROUND EATING NEW FOODS

As Nederkoorn et al. (2015) and Harpster et al. (2015) have indicated, there is a link between the feel of food and the way in which eating food is experienced. To help children become comfortable around new foods, it can help them to be able to explore the food in a more play-like way *before* they are encouraged to eat the food.

Activity 1 – Explore new foods

Toddlers can be given a few pieces of a new food or a small bowl of a new food to explore whilst they are playing. The bowl or plate can be placed next to them between the two of you. You can model picking up or touching the food as well as smelling it. Make sure that you use a bowl or plate that signifies that the items are edible. Talk about the food and what it feels like, smells like and what you know it tastes like. Ask your toddler if they would like to feed you a piece/spoonful of the food, talk about what it felt like in your mouth, even if it is a bit strange! Ask your toddler what noise they can make with their mouth when the food is in their mouth. For example, carrots make a crunching noise when bitten, but porridge does not. However, sucking porridge can make a glooping sound.

Activity 2 – Involve your child in preparing new foods

Even very young children can be involved in making food, whether it is putting ready-chopped or weighed ingredients in a bowl, or stirring, or pressing a button on a food processor. As they get older, they can do more and more steps, including growing and harvesting fruit and vegetables and then preparing and serving these. Be sensitive to your child's sensory needs and find work-arounds. For example, if you are chopping fruit for a fruit salad and your child does not like the texture of kiwi fruit, you may chop those and they chop the bananas.

Stirring mixtures is a part of preparing new foods and can help children to understand that there are many steps to making much of the food we eat. In addition, this provides very concrete learning around the way food changes as it is prepared. Eggs are completely different raw to cooked by themselves or mixed with other ingredients.

Activity 3 – Eating is fun!

When families sit down at a table or eating-mat together to eat, they can create wonderful memories and associations of a sense of belonging and warmth. If your child is eating by themselves, they may struggle to eat alongside others in the future, for example at school. Family mealtimes can be fun if the children are involved and the adults are as relaxed as possible about the process. Assign tasks to everyone in the family – even toddlers can put cutlery on the table to match cutlery outlines drawn on place mats in permanent marker. Breakfast is less likely to be fun as family members may be rushing to be somewhere or do something, so start with the evening meal as the fun activity.

You could plan a family evening picnic – each person gets to choose one thing to be included in the picnic (you may use a choice board of possible items for inclusion) and then the family shares these whilst relaxed and happy. If your family normally use cutlery, you can incorporate this, whereas if you usually eat with your fingers, you can offer cutlery or to feed a child if this helps them to try new food (without having to touch it).

Another fun activity is to watch some food preparation videos and then follow one of the videos as a family and compare your creation to that on the video! There are also many websites with visual picture recipes for children and adults who are not able to follow written instructions. Some of these can be printed and/or viewed as a step-by-step slideshow.

Activity 4 – Giving your child a choice

If you routinely offer to make a different meal for your child, you need to be willing to do this for their entire life! If not, you can use choice in a different way to empower your child. You can give them a choice of a tiny piece/serving (where effectively they are simply trying a bite-sized piece of a food to see if they like it yet, or not yet) or a medium-sized piece/serving. Both choices can be followed up with the choice of having more, if there is any, or not having any more. It is important to be very clear that it is fine not to like food, but that tastes change over time and that a food that you or they do not like now may be a favourite in a week/month/year's time, and this is why it is good to keep having a *tiny* taste, to see if your child/you like it *yet*!

You can use choice boards for this activity with a drawing or photo of their plate or bowl, and a drawing/photo of the meal or each item in the meal in tiny and medium servings. Your child can then simply point to the serving size they would like. You *must* respect their choice if you offer this and, similarly, *you* must have a tiny serving of anything on offer.

Other choices could be that one item can be refused per meal, or each person can choose which colour plate their food is served on.

Activity 5 – Eating in new places

Take familiar food to new places or order recognisable food that you know your child likes. Share food with your child, rather than requiring them to eat a whole meal. Stay relaxed about the experience and talk through what is different about the new place. Once your child is used to going to different places to eat, they will have developed an understanding of the concept of going out to eat or eating at someone else's house and this will no longer be as unpredictable.

Back up plans: ensure that your child is introduced to water as a drink when they are very young. Take a drink bottle with water in it wherever you go, prompt your child to drink regularly and make sure that they see you drinking water regularly. Talk about why people (and other animals) need to drink water to stay healthy.

GOING TO A NEW ENVIRONMENT

Autistic children vary in their ability to be comfortable in new environments. While, for some, going somewhere new results in major distress and meltdowns, for others, new environments are tolerated well. Generally, it is beneficial to be aware of the potential difficulties around new places, particularly with very young children, and to help them get used to experiencing new and different places. As with any change, preparing your autistic child for exposure to a new place, with new objects, smells, sounds and people, is an important step to ensure that his world is larger than your house/home. Some new places may be okay and others may not. There are a number of reasons for this, but there can seem to be no rhyme or reason as to why a child will happily go to the park but be terrified of the hairdresser.

For autistic people, the physical environment is often a significant contributor to either a sense of well-being or a sense of fear and confusion. Add the issue of all the sensory and social differences in a new place to reluctance and fear of unpredictability, and new places can be triggering and frightening to an autistic child.

Your child will need to go to new places as they travel through life. If every new place comes as a surprise and results in meltdowns, shutdowns or extreme anxiety, this can mean that the child increasingly associates new places with overload and stress and may become less and less confident about going to new places. The key is understanding the reason your child struggles with certain places, in addition to supporting and preparing them for each new environment and, in turn, supporting them to be able to go to new places with less fear and stress and to build up their confidence in going to new places:

> I grew up moving around. By the time I was 8, I had already lived in four countries in three continents and in over eight homes. To me, moving house was a normal and predictable event as, later, was changing schools. However, I hadn't been to a supermarket or seen snow until I was about 7. Both these new things were upsetting and overwhelming. My parents didn't tell me snow was cold and I had no reference point for that; I was so upset that it was cold! They had no idea that I didn't know it was cold as it was obvious to them that snow is cold. I think if I could tell parents of all children something, it would be that just because something is obvious to you, does not mean that it will be to your child. Please tell your children the details about where they are going, what they will see, hear, smell, touch, etc. It is so helpful to know what to expect. (Amy)

PREFERRED OUTCOMES AROUND GOING TO A NEW ENVIRONMENT

Some signs that your child is doing well with going into a new environment include:

- Your child is able to go to a range of different places and be confident and comfortable in themselves both on the way and once they have reached the destination.

- They do not have noticeably more meltdowns or shutdowns on the way to, or in new places.

- Your child does not get extremely stressed or anxious when you mention going to a new place.

- When your child is going to, or has just left a new place, they are largely their usual self, not more withdrawn, stressed or aggressive than usual.

- There is less or no pushback when you explain that you are going somewhere new with your child.

- If you make a Social Story™ or role play with favourite toys to explain going to the new place, your child responds positively or neutrally without demonstrating high anxiety or negativity about the place. This may be through talking or by clear non-verbal responses such as engaging with the story or role play rather than running away.

- Your child either communicates that they enjoyed time spent in a new place or it is evident in their demeanour (however, a meltdown or shutdown can occur after a positive experience, but be due to being overwhelmed with new stimuli/experiences).

- Your child requests or suggests a trip to somewhere that isn't home (e.g. to their grandparents' house).

- Your child visibly enjoys a trip to a new place, even if when they get there at first they are anxious or overwhelmed.

ACTIVITIES AROUND GOING TO A NEW ENVIRONMENT

Activity 1 – Visiting relatives

While spending time with extended family can be enjoyable and form an important part of a young child's social development, for autistic children, visiting grandparents, cousins or other family, or close family friends can be very challenging. The new environment of a different house, new smells and sounds and people can be stressful. Children with prosopagnosia (face blindness) can become very anxious if they know they are expected to recognise Grandma but they don't. Another issue can be around different sorts of 'rules' and customs among relatives. Grandparents especially can have considerably more relaxed or stricter attitudes around behaviour and boundaries, which can be confusing for autistic children. Sometimes, extended family members will bully or invalidate an autistic child, and there can be underlying issues around relatives not recognising autism as a genuine diagnosis and challenging parents on this. While this primarily presents a problem to parents of autistic children, the attitudes and feelings around it can be picked up on by autistic kids, who are often highly receptive to conflict and the emotions of others.

Visits to relatives often occur during holidays such as Christmas, New Year or family birthdays, weddings and so on. While children are usually expected to enjoy these events, they can also be overwhelming and cause overload and meltdown or shutdown. If this has occurred in the past, the child may associate relatives with meltdowns and overload and will be that much more anxious about attending family events. This in turn can set up a cycle of anxiety and avoidance, with the child refusing to go to the relatives' house, or visiting the relative but struggling to cope with the anxiety.

PREFERRED OUTCOMES: YOUR CHILD IS ABLE TO VISIT RELATIVES WITHOUT HUGE AMOUNTS OF STRESS FOR THEM OR YOU

Some signs that your child is doing well at visiting relatives include:

- They have either no, or a decreasing number and reduced intensity of, negative responses (e.g. meltdown or shutdown or distress) to visiting relatives.

- Your child is able to express some enjoyment at family events.

- Your child engages with extended family members in some way (e.g. conversation with Grandma, playing with or alongside cousins, etc.).

- Your child is able to articulate to parents or relatives in some way that they are anxious or overloaded.

- Your child can be calm while at relatives' houses, if only for short periods (noting that 'calm' varies for different children).

- Your child finds enjoyable things at the relatives' house (e.g. a cat to play with, an interesting plant in the garden, books to read or look at).

- Your child requests visits to relatives.

Autistic children can often become anxious if the adults or peers with them are anxious. So, if you as a parent are anxious about visiting family because your child is autistic and you are worried about what might happen, your child is more likely to become anxious and therefore more likely to become overloaded and have a shutdown or meltdown. The following activities will help you as a parent to be more confident about visiting relatives, as well as building resilience for your child/ren to visit relatives.

ACTIVITIES TO BUILD RESILIENCE FOR VISITING RELATIVES

Activity 1 – Looking at photos or videos of relatives

Although many children with prosopagnosia will be unable to recognise a person from their photo, looking at photos or videos of relatives can help to bring a sense of familiarity and an awareness of there being a positive connection to those people. When looking at the photos or videos, you want to talk about the people in them in a warm and positive manner, describing things that you have done with those relatives in the past. The idea is to create a sense of security for your child – that these are people you like and trust.

Activity 2 – Video chat with the relatives (child does not have to chat!)

By video chatting with your relatives, your child is able to see and hear their relatives in the comfort and security of their own home. They do not need to chat and initially may not even want to be on camera, but positioned so they can see and hear without being seen. Over time, you can encourage your child to greet (waving or smiling or saying 'hi') the relatives and share something with them on camera, such as holding up a drawing they have done or letting the relatives watch them playing over the video. When relatives ask questions of your child, give your child time to process the question and, if they are not responding, you can model a response. If your child does not use speech, make sure that your child has access to other forms of communication and, if need be, translate for your relatives, and together with your child teach the relatives how to understand the type of communication your child uses (e.g. sign or PECS or choice boards).

Activity 3 – Plan a short visit by relatives and share photos of their home and the environment around their home

Relatives appearing at your home may be less stressful for some autistic children than visiting the relatives in their home. Children should get used to visitors and visiting others when they are quite young so that they do not develop severe anxiety around this. However, visits may need to be quite short or your child should be able to be apart from the wider group for periods of time. Looking at photos of where the relatives live before you go there can help the child to predict what they will experience when they visit. If the relatives share some time with your child that is focused on their interest or passion, it should help your child to view the relatives in a positive manner.

Activity 4 – Plan and go on a short visit to relatives

Make sure that the planning is shared with your child using photos and a calendar (and even a timer – but if you say it will be half an hour or less, then make sure you leave within 30 minutes or your child will lose trust in you). Explore the different routes that you could take on the map – plan to go one way and come back a different way if possible so that your child does not become certain that there is only one way to get to that destination and only one way back. Make sure your child has a safe, quiet space to go to should they need to. Talk to relatives beforehand to ensure the room your child is staying in can be available to your child when they need to be in there. You can make a 'Do not disturb' sign for your child to hang up on the door when they do not want to be interrupted.

Activity 5 – Plan and go on an overnight visit to relatives

In this planning activity, you will also need to involve your child in packing an overnight case (if they are older than about 18 months!). You can help your child as much or as little as they need; use a packing list of essential items and then allow them to pick one to three other things to take with them that they want. Ensure that they understand that they are responsible for packing these things to come home again. Use the calendar and a map (paper or electronic) to show when you are going and when you are coming back. Explore the different routes that you could take on the map, including looking at the ways you went last time if it is a trip to the same relatives – plan to go one way and come back a different way if possible so that your child does not become certain that there is only one way to get to that destination and only one way back.

Activity 6 – Plan and go on a holiday to relatives for more than a couple of days

As per Activity 5, but packing requires more items and you will need to share some ideas of possible activities that will occur during the holiday. It is important to be very clear that planned activities may not happen, for example a picnic may be cancelled if it rains, a trip to the beach cancelled if there is a pollution alert and so on. This is necessary because many autistic children do not deal with disappointment or perceived unfairness very well. They often think that someone is just being mean or unfair if a planned activity is cancelled as they do not find it easy to understand the cause and effect of things that are not made explicit to them.

Ensure that your child has a favourite toy or book or music with them so that they have access to something that brings them calm/happiness fairly quickly, if needed.

Note – if your child is comfortable around particular relatives, you could encourage them to visit or stay with these relatives for a few hours, and then overnight, by themselves or with a sibling, but without you. If you do this, ensure that they know and have a visual reminder of when you are coming back to collect them.

Activity 7 – Preparing relatives for your child's visit

Relatives can be unpredictable in terms of their views around autism. You might have done everything you can do to prepare your child for their visit, but this can be undone by one poorly considered action or statement by a relative.

Things relatives should be aware of include:

- Your child's food likes and dislikes. Note that some older people might be of the opinion that a child should eat everything on their plate before they can leave the table. If your relatives think like this, it is important to discuss autism and food and how your child is not being deliberately fussy or picky.

- Understanding what meltdowns are and, more importantly, what the triggers for overload and meltdown are for your child. You can also let relatives know some information on autism generally, such as that meltdowns are not the same as tantrums and they are a response to overload and not a demand for an action (like a tantrum is).

- Talk about your child's interests with relatives. This can mean a connection is formed between your child and relatives based around interests. It can also make babysitting your child easier as they are likely to be engrossed in their interests.

As the following story from Russell demonstrates, it is important that your child knows when they will be returning home, and indeed when you will return if you leave them with their relatives:

I used to stay with my Nana and Grandpa a lot, and I loved being at their house, they had a huge vegetable garden, and I could go and pick things there. Usually, Mum stayed with me, but as I got a bit older, she would leave me there. I remember the first time she left me there after I had started school. She didn't tell me when she was coming back, and I was so upset. After two days, I got really, really anxious that she was never coming back to get me, even though Nana said she would, as Nana didn't tell me when. (Russell)

SPENDING TIME WITH ADULTS OTHER THAN PARENTS

There are two elements to this life event – that of the child being with adults other than parents but with their parents present, and that of being with adults other than parents when their parents are not present. The issues involved here include that of meeting new people but also the issue of trust. Adults other than parents can do unexpected things, speak differently, smell different, ask children things that seem to be odd or confusing requests, and impose rules and discipline about things that the child's parents do not impose rules and discipline about. They might speak in a different manner and have different attitudes towards interacting with children.

For very young autistic children, being left with a babysitter, childcare worker or relative while parents go out can be confusing and frightening. This confusion and anxiety can result in meltdown, anxiety and/or unhelpful behaviours such as aggression, which can lead to a range of negative consequences for the child and their parents. Many parents of young autistic children simply do not go out as a couple due to concerns around getting an appropriate babysitter, which can put strain on relationships and have an impact on their relationship with their child as well. However, all children go through a phase of being afraid of strangers, often being completely unafraid before and/or after. What you are aiming to do is enable your child to be comfortable around other adults and for them to be sure that *you* will respond to anything that they are unsure about in their interactions with other adults.

Preferred outcomes: Your child can be left with a trusted babysitter or childcare worker without any extra stress for you or your child.

Some indicators that your child is doing well at spending time with adults other than parents include:

- Your child's behaviour is not aggressive or combative and defiant when introduced to – or left with – an adult other than a parent.

- Spending time with adults other than parents does not consistently cause your child extreme anxiety.

- Your child's ability to spend time with adults other than parents improves over time.

- After some practice, parents are able to spend evenings or other times out by themselves and are mostly confident that their child will manage with a babysitter.

It is easiest to start these activities *after* you have done Activities 1–3 around visiting relatives.

Activity 1 – Having new adults in the house

If you have family friends who you are really comfortable around, you may well have had them visit your house since before your child/ren was/were born, in which case, you have already done this activity. However, if you have not had friends in your home for quite some time, then you need to do so. Even taking your child to the door when you open it for a courier or delivery is helpful for building resilience around new adults. Obviously, you will not have photos of these types of people, but for family friends, you can ask them if you can share their photos with your child before they visit. When you share the photo, explaining that this person is coming later on today, tell your child more about the person. Do they have any characteristics that will help your child to identify them? What is it that you really like about this friend? It is important that you control the situation and not your child. If your child is uncomfortable, accept and validate that by letting them know that meeting new people can be difficult, and you are so pleased that they are managing the situation so well. Do *not* ask your friend to leave if your child has a meltdown. If you can see a meltdown coming, guide your child to their safe space and/or calming activity. Wait until after your child is calm to say goodbye to your friend. You do not want your child to learn that they can control the entire family by screaming/crying/becoming aggressive. Instead, you want to help your child to understand that even though meltdowns may happen, they signal situations to learn to manage, and that neither you nor they should be embarrassed or ashamed of struggling to manage.

If your child screams or lashes out as soon as they see someone entering your home, you still need to have people come into the house, but you would want them to do so initially when your child is in their safe space and/or engaged in an activity they enjoy. In this case, you do not need the visitor to interact or even see your child, just let them be able to be heard and seen briefly by your child.

Activity 2 – Being alone in a room at home with an adult for a short period of time

This activity needs you/a parent to still be at home with your child.

You do not want to do this activity until your child is comfortable with Activity 1 around having adults visit your house.

Depending on your child, you can do this activity in one of two ways:

1. Being very explicit about the fact that you are leaving the room to go to another room and that the other adult will stay in the room with the child.

2. Being completely involved in a preferred activity with the other adult and your child and then quietly leaving the activity and moving around within sight of your child and coming back, then leaving the room briefly and returning with a snack/drink for everyone (if your child likes snacks/drinks). Each time you leave the room, stay away a little longer, but on the first day that you do this, be guided by the anxiety levels of your child – that is, stop leaving if their anxiety builds.

Activity 3 – Being alone with an adult at home

For this activity, you will need to be explicit about how long you are going to be away and when you are coming back. Make sure your child has something to do that they enjoy so they are focused on their activity that they are not continually worrying about when you are coming back. You can make a visual of:

*   **first**: your child and the adult in the house and

*   **then**: you, your child and the adult in the house, and

*   **later**: you and your child in the house (and any other family members who will be returning home) – you can use photos or drawings, depending on which your child is more comfortable with.

Activity 4 – Visiting a childcare centre after hours to meet a childcare worker

Childcare centres can initially be very overwhelming for autistic children, particularly if they are only children or have had minimal contact with other children and non-family member adults. For this reason, it is best to visit before the children arrive or after they leave on your first visit. Discuss this with the centre director/manager and explain why you want to do this.

During this discussion, share some of your child's interests and how they communicate. Ask if the person from the childcare centre who meets you and your child can greet your child warmly and then ask them about their interest or share an item or book with them that relates to that interest/ passion. This will ensure that your child feels welcomed and valued and set up the relationship for success.

MEETING OTHER CHILDREN

Meeting other children can be very stressful for autistic children for a number of reasons. These include:

- *The unpredictability of children.* Many autistic children are happier being around adults than children because they are more likely to conform to similar patterns of behaviour, whereas other children can do unexpected things like cry, be aggressive, play confusing games and expect the autistic child to join in with things they do not understand or find interesting or enjoyable.

- *Change.* In a childcare, kindergarten or school setting, there are many changes that occur which can leave autistic children anxious and confused. Many of these changes relate to the other children. They can be away unexpectedly, be off sick for some time and come back as the centre of attention. They might leave altogether without anyone explaining to the autistic child why they left.

- *Children can be bullies and aggressive, and can pick on the autistic child.* Not only is this frightening when it is happening, but it can also lead the autistic child to start on a journey of self-doubt, self-loathing and questioning who they are, which can continue into adulthood.

- *Allegiances with small children are often quite fluid.* This is an issue that autistic people can face throughout their lifetime. They may be friends with a child one day and the next day the child loses interest or doesn't want to be friends anymore. For autistic children, this can be very confusing – they were friends yesterday, so why aren't they friends now?

When I started pre-school, I was 3, and I could read. I wanted to learn to write, and I wasn't interested in all the other kids at all. They all wanted to play with all these toys and things, but I just wanted to learn to write and to read books. I loved books. I don't remember ever having friends at any of my pre-schools, but I do remember the teachers. Actually, I don't even remember the other kids; just that I didn't want to do the things that they were doing. (Amy)

Meeting and interacting with other children can be very hard, but there are strategies that can assist with addressing this and building your child's social resilience. You may find that your child is more or less interested in children than adults. It is easier to build interest in children if there is a common or shared interest between your child and another child. This is why groups or clubs can be useful, even for toddlers. For example, if you have a toddler who loves to climb and jump, you may join a toddler gymnastics group. There, the other toddlers will also be doing things that your child likes, so they will automatically be feeling more at ease than they would be if the other children were doing things they didn't enjoy or understand.

PREFERRED OUTCOMES: YOUR CHILD IS COMFORTABLE IN THEMSELVES AROUND OTHER CHILDREN

Some indicators that your child is doing well in meeting and interacting with other children include:

- No or infrequent calls from childcare or school about victimisation of your child by peers or aggression towards other children or other challenging behaviour by your child.

- Your child talks about a child or other children at kindergarten, childcare or school in a positive or interested way.

- Your child has a friend around their own age or children they enjoy playing with.

- Your child is either willing or not oppositional about attending childcare, kindergarten or school.

- Your child asks to visit or play with another child.

- If your child has imaginary play, that play includes characters who are children of a similar age.

- Your child is invited to birthday parties of their peers.

It is important to remember that not all autistic children do/don't engage in imaginary play and that usually they prefer to play alongside peers rather than with peers for most of their pre-school years.

Activity 1 – Watching TV or videos about other children

You can help your child to understand other children by describing what they are doing and possible reasons why. This can be done more easily by watching a video or TV show together that has children in it. You can introduce the idea that some people are nice and kind and that some people are not good friends. This is important as autistic children tend to trust everyone or no-one without explicit teaching about the difference between positive and negative relationships of all kinds.

Activity 2 – Having relatives with children visit for a short period of time

Set up some parallel play activities – these are activities where both children are able to play next to one another without having to actually interact with one another. This means that you need to have two toy cars, for example, one for each child, as they will play with their own car rather than interact with the other child and their car. Drawing, Play-Doh and puzzles are other activities that are easy to set up parallel play opportunities with.

Activity 3 – Go to a group/club that shares an interest with your child (or an autistic children's club/group)

This activity is very dependent upon your child: if they like to climb and jump, you may want to take them to a trampoline or gymnastics for toddlers group/club. Other children may prefer a Lego group or a dance session or story-time at your local library. Do *not* expect your child to join in on their first visit and be very explicit that they can watch the other children and/or join in with the activity, whichever they are comfortable doing. Some autistic children need to watch an activity for a number of times before they are comfortable joining in, whilst others will join in much more quickly:

> My parents belonged to a theatre group when I was 4–6 years old. I loved going there with them. I learnt all the lines for all the plays and could be the group prompter. I didn't know how unusual this was until I was in my 30s. I think sometimes families limit their autistic children because they want them to be just like other kids. I didn't want to play with other kids. It made me happy being at the theatre. (Amy)

STARTING CHILDCARE/KINDERGARTEN/ PRIMARY SCHOOL

For many children, going to childcare, kindergarten or primary school for the first time is very challenging. For autistic children, this transition can be particularly difficult. Childcare or school may be the first time a child is exposed to large groups of other children. Primary school can be particularly difficult due to there being a large range of ages at school, with the eldest students being 11 or 12 years old. School or daycare can result in overload and meltdowns. It can also result in bullying by other students. The new routine and strange environment can be overwhelming for autistic children even if the other kids are being respectful and inclusive.

In school, the curriculum and in childcare, play-based learning can be confusing. There may seem to be no routine, with different teachers and administration and support staff, assemblies, sports activities and concerts making the environment unpredictable. This lack of predictability can eat away at the autistic child's sense of security and safety and this can lead to behavioural issues and a very stressed and unhappy child.

A child's initial experiences or learning, socialising and fitting in with the routine and structure of the day at childcare, kindergarten or school can dictate how they experience education – and even employment – in later life. It is very important to plan for your child's transition to part-time or full-time childcare/pre-school and/or school. This planning is as much for you as it is for your child and the childcare workers and educators involved. Try to stay as calm and relaxed about the transition as possible, as your child will sense your anxiety if you are anxious and it will affect their attitude to the transition, even if this is subconscious.

Autistic children often face some challenges in attending childcare, kindergarten or school, some of which are shared by many of their non-autistic peers. These include things like:

- missing their parent/s

- being in a new and strange place

- getting used to routines and classes

- learning new information

- meeting other students and experiencing the social dynamics in school and where they fit within it.

Autistic children can also experience some challenges that are more specific to autism. These issues may not be picked up on by support staff or teachers. They include:

- sensory issues and challenges

- being in a new, untested, confusing place

- frustration at not being able to master skills immediately

- learning a whole new area of social communication outside of the family home

- being overwhelmed by social expectations and contact with other children

- difficulties with assimilating the new routine

- difficulties understanding why other children and adults' movements change.

Starting childcare, kindergarten or school is often a huge challenge for autistic kids, so preparation and support are vital. It is likely that there will be some issues with meltdowns and/or distress when your child attends for the first time, but this does not mean that each day will be just as difficult. Each child has a different timeframe for managing a big transition like this, but you can assist your child to get a more positive experience from these kinds of transitions and build their confidence for transitions in the future. Ensuring your child feels welcomed and valued by engaging in the activity of spending time with other adults with each new key childcare worker/teacher will set up the transition to be less stressful and less anxiety-provoking for your child.

If these transition points can be made to be less stressful and confusing through transition planning and explicit communication between you and your child, this can have a big impact on your child's resilience and independence throughout their life. The transition from family group to social/peer group at childcare or school may be the first time your child is in a social setting with peers of their own age. Therefore, this is a really important transition to support your child through in order to give them skills for managing social situations and approaching and interacting with other children from a place of resilience.

Many autistic children do not understand the point of childcare, pre-school or school unless it is made explicit by their family members. This seems to be particularly problematic long term if children do not understand that children go to school to learn new skills and knowledge. If you yourself did not enjoy school or pre-school, it is worth visiting by yourself initially and talking to staff members about what children do in these settings these days, as education has changed dramatically in the past 10 years!

Preferred outcomes: That you and your child manage the transition to childcare, kindergarten and then school with minimal stress and some level of excitement and positivity about what your child may learn at that place.

The outcomes around transition to childcare, kindergarten or school can vary significantly across different children. Do not worry if it takes your child longer to settle into a new setting than another child. Approximately six weeks is common for children to settle down and get used to their new environment, however, this can be significantly longer for some children.

Some indicators that your child is managing the transition well include:

- Your child does not regularly have meltdowns or refuse to attend school or childcare.

- Behaviour at home does not consistently become markedly more challenging after your child has been going to school or childcare for some weeks or months.

- Your child has positive stories to tell about their day when they come home.

- Your child expresses that they are looking forward to an event at school/childcare.

- Your child makes a friend (although many autistic children struggle to maintain friendships when they are very young, or conversely think that everyone who ever speaks to them is a friend).

- Your child expresses positive thoughts about childcare or school or an element of it (e.g. a particular teacher or support worker they like or a subject they enjoy).

- Few or no disciplinary incidents, or, if there is a disciplinary incident, it is due to a teacher or support childcare worker misunderstanding your child's behaviour and not, in fact, due to any actual poor behaviour.

Activity 1 – Visit the new setting when it is closed to walk around and take photos

The physical environment can impact on an autistic child's sense of well-being. New environments may be anxiety-provoking in and of themselves, even without the other stresses of school or childcare like new people and routines. Contact the school or childcare centre and obtain permission to take your child to their new school or childcare centre after hours, when there are no children there, and show them the different areas they will be going to – their classroom, the toilets, the reception desk, playground and so on. This will help to alleviate one significant stressor around starting at a new school or childcare centre. Let your child explore the space – sit on the chairs, touch the walls, investigate the playground. This will help give your child more confidence when they go to school or childcare 'for real'. You can stagger going to childcare by going for a part-day, a few days a week, and increasing the length of time and number of days.

Activity 2 – Create a transition video or book

You can make a book or video that explains to your child different aspects of going to school or childcare. You can use family members and other people your child knows and trusts as the characters in the story. Your book or video could set out things that happen when your child will go to school or childcare for the first time. If you know your child is anxious about one element of starting school or childcare (meeting the teacher, knowing what to do with their bag, etc.), you can focus on this in the story. After they have seen the book or video, encourage your child to ask questions about anything in the narrative or anything they are concerned about that you may have missed. Your child may need to look at the story a few times. They might want something added. If this is the case, work with them to include the new element. The story will work well if it is interactive and your child engages with it. You can share the story with your child's teacher/childcare worker too and they can help your child relate the content of the book to the reality of school or childcare.

Activity 3 – Celebrate the first part-day visit

Marking and celebrating milestones is a great motivator and not just for small children. In the lead-up to your child's first part-day visit at their new school, talk to them about what the visit will involve. Prepare a celebration to mark their first part-day visit and involve your child in this. While some parenting advice focuses on sanctions for poor behaviour, this is quite often counterproductive and particularly for autistic children, whose 'errors' may be unintentional. The positive reinforcement of a planned celebration is a great way to build resilience in your child. Plan the event with them – and it doesn't need to be big or expensive. As much as possible, make your messaging around their school visit positive. Ask questions about what your child is looking forward to doing at school. You can offer some suggestions of your own about potential positive experiences that can happen at school.

If in fact they have a difficult time and come home feeling they have failed, still have the celebration because they attended. However, take the opportunity to talk to them about the part-day and help plan strategies for their next visit to school. Stay as positive as you can but do not gloss over issues – use them instead to help your child move on from a setback. When the time comes for the first full-day visit to school, put in place a similar process of celebration. Focus on positives and reward the effort of attending school for a whole day.

Many primary schools are happy for parent interaction with the children. You being in your child's classroom can help with transitions or difficult times at school.

Activity 4 – Celebrate the first whole week at school or childcare

You can plan a celebration for when your child attends their first full week of school. Give your child some agency by allowing them to decide the theme and/or other elements of the celebration as much as possible. Consciously explain to your child that the celebration is for them completing a full week at school. However, do not cancel it if they fall a bit short of the goal and only attend three or four full days or a number of part-days. Focus on what they have achieved and how they can achieve more. While you should not simply cancel the celebration if your child does not achieve the full week of attendance, when you are speaking to your child before and during the first week of school, don't mention that the celebration will happen even if they only attend for part of the week. Keep your child focused on the goal of a full week of attendance.

Be aware that meltdown, shutdown and overload can happen in response to positive situations, too. Help your child to de-escalate by removing stimuli such as talking, noise, visual or other sensory stimuli. Avoid physical contact, unless your child finds hard hugging helpful when they are overloaded. If a meltdown or shutdown does occur, do not punish your child for this — it is likely they were just as upset that it occurred as you are — or more so.

Activity 5 – Make school attendance fun

You can make school attendance fun. This can be particularly helpful for children who enjoy games and competitions. You can set attendance goals or learning goals for your child and then turn them into a game where they improve or build on previous performance. You can get quite creative and make up cards for which school-related, learning, behavioural or social activity your child can focus on this week. With young children, make sure that any competition is just between your child and him or herself rather than with a friend or sibling. Make sure that the competitive nature of the activity is always described as fun and not serious, and that 'winning' is less the goal than improving or building on previous outcomes. These sorts of methods around building skills in all areas of school and education can be adapted for older children, too. Note that some children become overly anxious around competitions and challenges, even those where they aren't competing with anyone else. If this describes your child, it might be better to simply set goals rather than asking them to try to compete against themselves to improve their performance.

Another way to make school attendance fun is to help your child and their teacher share fun moments. For example, if your child has a great sense of humour, encourage them to use this appropriately with their teacher to bring a smile to their teacher. Most autistic children do not want to be around people who they feel do not like them, so it is important for them to feel that their teacher likes them. If you give their teacher a picture/book/toy that is linked to one of your child's passions/interests, the teacher can greet your child with that on days that your child has been reluctant to attend school. This simple strategy is surprisingly effective at helping children see school positively.

HAVING A NEW SIBLING

The birth of a new baby can be challenging for any older sibling but for autistic kids it can be a particularly traumatic and difficult time. A new baby means another person in the house – and if the autistic older brother or sister has not been around babies much, then routine things like the baby crying, feeding and needing changing can be confusing and difficult to manage. For very young children and those who are non-verbal and don't have effective communication aids, it can be hard for them to express their concerns and issues with having a new baby around. This can result in overload, meltdowns and even aggressive behaviour.

For some autistic children, they may be excited about the arrival of the baby and be fascinated by the physiological changes their mother is going through, but may not be prepared for the reality of having a baby brother or sister.

A baby takes parental attention and time away from the older sibling, which can result in a lot of trauma, sometimes leading to jealousy and sibling rivalry that can continue into adulthood in some instances.

Preparation is key with this type of major change. You cannot send the baby back or give the baby away just because their older sibling would like this to occur. So, whatever the response from the older brother or sister is, the baby is staying. This means that interventions and supports cannot include the avoidance option.

While bringing a new baby home can result in a negative response, the opposite can also be true. Some autistic children may be wonderful older siblings to a baby and having a little brother or sister can enable others to see their loving and caring side. Whatever the response, though, having a new baby is almost always going to result in significant disruption to routines and family dynamics. Equipping your autistic child with as much information as you can prior to the baby coming home is a helpful strategy:

> I was nearly 8 when my baby brother was born. I knew that Mum was having a baby, and I had decided it would be really good to have a little sister to look after. I didn't want another brother, because I already had a brother and in my mind all brothers would be the same. Which in this case meant that all brothers would destroy my teddy bears. When my grandparents got the phone call to say Mum had the baby, they excitedly told me I had a new brother, and I cried and cried

and cried because I was so disappointed that I didn't have a sister! My grandparents were really angry with me, because it was supposedly a happy occasion. I wish I had known that it might be a boy or a girl and that my wanting one or the other did not mean that that would happen. (Lara)

Preferred outcomes: That your autistic child accepts and values their younger sibling.

It is likely that it will take a while for the disruption caused by bringing home a new baby to settle down. Given that this is a fairly major disruption for your autistic child, the preferred outcomes may take a while to eventuate. Many children regress in some of their skills and behaviours when a new sibling is born. This is quite typical and does not mean that your child will permanently lose those skills. Children who are very aware of and involved in the upcoming changes are less likely to regress, but may still do so.

Some indicators that your child is managing this significant change well include:

- They talk to the baby and include them in their games (e.g. talking about the baby as a character in their play 'world' or playing alongside the baby so baby can see and hear what they are doing).

- Your child's behaviour gets back to a similar point to before the baby was born.

- Your child includes the baby in their drawings of the family in a way that depicts positivity (smiling, etc.).

- Social Stories™ you may have used to support the transition of bringing the baby home work effectively.

- Your child asks to help you look after the baby or demonstrates caring behaviour.

ACTIVITIES TO PREPARE YOUR CHILD TO COPE WELL AND BE RESILIENT ABOUT HAVING A NEW SIBLING

Activity 1 – Answering questions

Encourage and answer any questions about pregnancy, childbirth or babies, regardless of whether you feel they are embarrassing or personal. Explain the process of pregnancy, childbirth and early childhood to your autistic child. You can do this using Social Stories™ or a similar narrative technique. Encourage questions and discussion around your pregnancy and what life will be like when the new baby arrives.

Activity 2 – Meeting babies

Some autistic children are confused by having a new baby around. They don't remember being a baby themselves and they are not quite sure what to do with this small person who cries and – at first – does not really interact much with the world. The autistic child might think the new baby will be helpless and small forever. This can be quite scary and confusing.

This activity involves introducing your child to babies at different stages of development. If you have friends or family members with babies at different ages, introduce your child to the babies and explain the processes of development. Encourage and answer any questions your child has. Explain that your child's brother or sister will also get older and be a child and then an adult. If you are worried about how your child may manage around a baby, you could buy a 'baby' doll, but be sure to explain that this is a doll and a real baby is very fragile and needs to be touched carefully or it might get hurt.

Activity 3 – Preparing to be a big brother or sister

Explain to your child how the baby will change things in your family but how your child will remain a really important part of the family too and their role as big brother or sister is just as important as the parents'. Look at books and videos about babies and siblings with your child. It can also help some children to have a baby doll before or shortly after the baby arrives. You can treat the doll as if it were your baby and demonstrate how to hold it and care for it. You can show your child how to be gentle with the baby using the doll. Learning how to hold the doll like a real baby will be useful, particularly if your child develops an awareness of the need to support the baby's neck. If your child is able to help wash the doll with the care and attention required for a real baby, they can help an adult with the baby's bath time. Some autistic children do not respond to dolls, so this approach will not work for all children, but it can be very effective for some.

Activity 4 – Being a responsible big brother or sister

Before the baby arrives, talk to your child about how to be a responsible brother or sister. Instead of focusing the discussion on the baby, talk about the qualities of a helpful, caring and kind older sibling and how pleased you will be when your child demonstrates those qualities. You can use a system of rewards for good sibling behaviour, whether these are things like stickers or reward charts or things like special one-on-one time with a parent or extra time to be engaged in their passion. It is important with all reward systems that you reward your child as much as possible to start off with and over time fade the rewards until they are only given periodically. If you do not fade rewards out, you can create a dependence on a reward for all desired behaviours.

Activity 5 – Managing jealousy and rivalry

Sibling rivalry can begin early for autistic children and it can impact on their sense of self-worth and security, which can lead to difficulties with being resilient and independent later in life. Jealousy and sibling rivalry can be difficult to address but if a parent is aware it is an issue they can put in place some strategies to help alleviate it.

This activity involves showing your child that they are an individual and that they are loved and cared for as much as the baby is. You may need to be very conscious of how your behaviour may be interpreted by your autistic child as they may think you are favouring their brother or sister. You can play a game with your child that involves you telling your autistic child a positive thing about them and then asking them to say something good about themselves. You can pass them a toy or something else they like as you say the positive thing. Then say something positive about the baby.

Do not make your child say a positive thing about their sibling if they don't want to but encourage them to identify something the baby might like or enjoy. This activity should be done when your child is calm and in a safe place. If sibling rivalry is an issue, reassure your autistic child that you love and care for them as well as their sister or brother. Every night, you can have some time just with your older child once the baby has been put in bed. During this time, you can remind your child how much babies change and develop over time.

Activity 6 – Sharing attention

Babies take a lot of time and energy, which can be interpreted by an older sibling as meaning that their parent/s don't want to spend time with them. This can cause significant anxiety and anger to older siblings, who can feel displaced by a new baby. Some children, not just autistic children, can regress when a baby arrives and temporarily lose some of their language and emotional skills.

Sibling rivalry can be explained by a number of different things, including your autistic child not understanding the needs of a baby and the time demands this places on parents.

Try to give attention to your autistic child when you can so as to enforce the message that the baby is not getting more love than them. This may not be possible if the baby is sick or if sleep is broken for long periods of time. Parents are human after all and being sleep-deprived and having an upset child and a screaming baby will try the patience of the most saintly parent! One way to help your older child understand why you are less available now, is to explain what you are doing with the baby when they take up your time.

Explain changing the baby and what it involves and why it needs to be done urgently. Older siblings can also learn how to change the baby and/or help out during changes by, for example, handing the clean nappy to the person doing the change. You can talk about feeding the baby and why you can talk to your other child whilst feeding but not do anything active at the same time as feeding the baby. If the baby is bottle-fed, older siblings can assist with this, too.

Reassure your autistic child that the fact your attention may be focused on the baby a lot is because little babies can't look after themselves;

the baby will get bigger and more able to do things for themselves, and your giving attention to the baby does not mean you don't love or care for your older child.

MANAGING BEING TOLD 'NO!'

Young children need to learn the limits to and consequences of what they do. Learning the meaning of 'no' and how to respond appropriately is vital for all children. A parental 'No!' can be for a number of reasons, including to warn of imminent danger, to express that the child cannot have something (e.g. an expensive toy), to discipline or address inappropriate behaviour or to express displeasure at an action the child is doing such as eating things that may hurt the child. For example, at 18 months, a child was eating sheep dung – certainly an opportune moment for an emphatic 'No!' Other common things children try and eat are dirt and sand.

'No!' is essentially a boundary or limit. Learning boundaries and limits is essential for all children – autistic or otherwise. Being secure in the knowledge of where boundaries are is a key element in optimal child development. 'No' may be met with some resistance from children and may be a lesson that takes a while to instil in your child, but responding appropriately to 'No!' and other boundaries is a vital skill to be learnt. A lot of helpful attitudes around behaviour and identity stem from that initial understanding as a child of the limit 'No!'. This is true for both autistic and non-autistic children.

Autistic children often need to understand 'No!' to a greater extent than other children, but it can sometimes be hard to get through. The younger your child is when you start to teach them 'No', 'Later' and 'Not yet', the better. Don't forget that the value of 'Yes' is diminished if there is never a 'No' to balance things out. To children, 'No!' may not be understood in the way the parent means it. One of the reasons for this is that in typical autistic-thinking style, the 'Now is forever', which means that if you are saying 'No' now, then you will always be saying no. For this reason, it can be helpful to provide clarity around the 'No'. For example, 'No, you can't stay up and watch TV any longer. You can watch more TV tomorrow.'

Autistic children may become hyperaware of approval and disapproval, so a parent saying 'No!' may be interpreted as a disapproval not only of their behaviour but of them as a person. Some autistic children do not have a good concept of risk or danger, so the parental 'No!' around, for example, them going towards a river with the intention of swimming when it is unsafe, may be meaningless and ignored. Some autistic children have other co-morbid conditions such as attention deficit hyperactivity disorder (ADHD) or oppositional defiance disorder (ODD), which can also have an impact on the child learning the value and meaning of 'No!'.

Despite the challenges, 'No!' is an incredibly important concept for children to assimilate, which has impacts on risk and safety, communication, boundaries and limits and, ultimately, independence. This is because a child that cannot respond appropriately to 'No!' in the home, will struggle to do so in school and later in the wider community. This can result in them being labelled as having inherently challenging behaviour, when really they just do not know how to accept boundaries. Being able to accept and respond to 'No!' is not the same as being completely compliant, rather it is about accepting the adult boundaries of what is safe and acceptable in the moment.

Preferred outcomes: Your autistic child may take longer than you expect to fully understand 'No!' and respond in a helpful way. It is also important to note that children at different ages may have significantly different responses to the boundary 'no'.

Some indicators that your child is successfully integrating their understanding of 'No!' into their life include:

- A decreasing number of times that 'No!' needs to be said and followed up by a parent.

- Decreasing levels of distress when a boundary is set.

- Some indication that your child understands the impact of not complying with the boundary (e.g. 'If I run away, I will get into trouble' or 'I'm not meant to run away because I might get hurt').

- Decreasing oppositional behaviour in response to 'No!'.

ACTIVITIES AROUND STATING LIMITS AND SAYING 'NO!'

Activity 1 – Learning consequences

Using Social Stories™, role plays or other narrative communication help your child to understand what the consequences of an action are. Do not assume that they will transfer their knowledge for different consequences, especially at first. You may need to create a different story for each activity and consequence. Get your child as engaged in this process as possible. The first couple of stories you may need to complete yourself and demonstrate to your child, but then you may be able to get your child to work out the actions and what they might lead to.

Young children tend to have difficulty understanding abstract concepts like danger or death, so relate the consequence to something your child knows – either an event in their life or a character in a TV programme, game or film they like. For example, to explain the concept of pain or injury you could say draw on memories of physical pain or injury. Other practical consequences such as what happens after breaking something also need to be learnt. If you replace something your child breaks too quickly, they will not understand why this does not happen at school, or why other people get upset or angry with them when they break things later in life.

Emotional consequences like sadness or shame vary considerably between children and are not as effective at teaching boundaries as practical consequences. Young children are quite capable of learning to take care of things if they see a reason to do so, whereas if they do not need to because broken things get replaced instantly, they will not learn this valuable lesson. This may be where you can teach 'no' in a way that teaches responsibility. For example, 'No, you cannot get a new train yet. You need to show me you know how to look after your trains first.'

Activity 2 – Strengthening understanding

Usually, when a parent says 'No!' it is in the heat of the moment and in response to a behaviour that needs to stop right away. With autistic children, they may try to unpack what is behind the 'no' – wondering, 'Does my parent hate me?', feeling acute anxiety, even at the tone and volume of the command and not understanding what it is they aren't meant to be doing. This can lead to the child having no idea what to do next. Their apparent poor listening and behaviour can actually just be due to them not understanding what is happening. So, for this activity, it can help to go back to before you even have to say 'no' to your child. This activity involves helping your child understand boundaries and discipline by working through what 'no' actually means, why you say it and so on. You can scaffold understanding for your child so that when 'No!' is said, they understand why, that they are okay, their parent doesn't hate them and it is just a normal part of life to be told 'no'.

In addition, it is not enough to tell your child what not to do: you also need to let them know what to do instead. For example, if you are going up to cross the road and you worry your child is about to run out into the road, you can say 'No, wait for me, we can cross together.' Once they wait, thank them for waiting and re-explain the dangers of running across a road.

Activity 3 – Understanding 'No!'

(This activity would be better suited to children aged over 5)

You can talk to your child about circumstances in which you might need to say 'No!' to them. You can have a role play with your child and you can pretend to be them and then ask them to play you. Set up some scenarios for the role play where the parent would need to say 'No!'. Ask your child to say 'No!' to you while in character and to explain what the 'No!' related to and why they needed to say it. Then, talk to them about why you might tell them 'no' in similar situations. As many autistic children love drama and role play, this game might be good fun as well as being helpful. Enjoyable activities tend to enable knowledge to be incorporated into a child's – or adult's – understanding a lot quicker than bland instruction.

SHARING WITH OTHERS AND TAKING TURNS

Sharing with others is another vital childhood skill. It is not only autistic children who can struggle with this. Sharing and taking turns are skills that may be acquired at different ages for different children. However, this skill can be particularly difficult for autistic children to understand due to the typical autistic thinking style of the 'now' being forever. Because of this, when it is your turn, your child thinks that they may never get a turn again!

The value of sharing for older children and adults is huge. Sharing and taking turns are a key part of communication and working together with others. Autistic children can learn to share and take turns just like other people can, with explicit teaching and role modelling. Having siblings or close cousins or family friends can be a useful resource for practising skills around sharing and taking turns. However, it is always better to teach turn-taking and sharing with an autistic child and one cooperative adult before practising with a larger group.

Autistic children may have some difficulties with sharing for a number of reasons. These include:

- *Not understanding the concept of sharing or taking turns.* Often, assumed knowledge is incorrectly applied to autistic children. When they don't comply with a certain expected behaviour, they are punished for it. However, they may not understand the concept, rather than being intentionally disobedient.

- *Some autistic children have objects – toys and so on – which they use for stimming and self-soothing.* These objects are very important to them and another child wanting to share is met with horror as the autistic child does not know if the special object will be returned by the other child or whether it will be broken or damaged when they get it back.

- *Some autistic children struggle to communicate with other children.* Sharing and taking turns requires a fair degree of skill at communication and reciprocity; the autistic child may learn these at a later age than their non-autistic peers.

- *The 'now is forever' thinking style.*

There are many largely unhelpful stereotypes that show autistic children as being selfish, lacking empathy, having no notion of being thoughtful and so on. These attitudes can follow autistic people into adulthood, with them being described as rude, aloof and/or thoughtless. These sorts of stereotypes are often based on a misunderstanding of how autistic people relate to the world. There is a lot of history to these beliefs on autism and they are often not very helpful. In fact, many autistic children are highly empathic and thoughtful, but this can manifest in different ways to how it does in typically developing children.

Sometimes, parents or adult carers can misinterpret what they see in regard to sharing. The autistic child may actually be playing inclusively but in fact be experiencing bullying from another child. The response to the bullying may be misinterpreted as a meltdown or some kind of selfish tantrum related to not sharing. As always with children – and particularly with autistic children – it is wise to work out exactly what has occurred before jumping to conclusions. In addition, parallel play, where two or more children are playing alongside each other with indirect engagement, is more common for autistic children of all ages, whereas other children tend to move more easily from parallel to joint or group play.

Parallel play has less stress for autistic children and young people as there is minimal social interaction between participants. This means that the child is able to focus on the play/game rather than stressing about the inherent interactions. For this reason, parallel play is important and valuable as it enables skill-building and confidence for autistic children in a less stressful manner. For example, children can learn to learn how to manage losing at a game by playing single player games and become comfortable and confident in their ability to lose and move on. Once they have mastered this skill, they can then start to integrate 'losing well' into play with others.

Every autistic child is an individual. Try to avoid assumptions around social communication and meet your child where they are at. This may involve using some more imaginative ways to build skills around sharing and taking turns that are specific to your child's needs. Please don't discount your child's turn-taking and sharing skills based on a few challenges or setbacks. It is important to skill-build turn-taking in a range of situations with different people as it is one thing to take turns with someone who does this fairly, and another to take turns with someone who does not respond in an expected or appropriate manner.

Preferred outcomes: As with many skills, your child's capacity for sharing and taking turns will most likely change and develop over time. Younger children may need to develop the skill more as they grow.

Some indicators of your child having acquired the skill or sharing and taking turns are:

- Decreasing distress, anxiety or meltdowns around sharing and taking turns.

- Friendships or parallel play with peers is developing.

- Your child is able to share toys and games with another child more frequently.

- Your child can articulate in whatever way they communicate that they do want to share something and why.

- Your child is less anxious about siblings or peers playing with their toys or being in 'their' space.

ACTIVITIES AROUND SHARING AND TAKING TURNS
Activity 1 – Sharing with your child

This activity involves showing your child that sharing can benefit them, too. For this activity, have something – a toy or game – that you know your child will enjoy and say to them, 'Would you like me to share this with you?' If they say, 'Yes,' allow your child to play with the toy. Make a little input to the play yourself to demonstrate that you are sharing and not giving. When the play finishes, ask your child for the toy or game back. Thank your child for returning the toy. If this stage is difficult, you may need to practice it a few times and reward your child for successful returning of the toy or game.

Once your child is confident in returning your toys, ask them to share one of their own toys with you. When you have finished playing, return the toy and thank your child for sharing. When a sibling or other child wants to share your child's toys or games, remind your child of how well they shared with you and relate the experience of them sharing with you to the other child. You can acknowledge how difficult sharing can be and reinforce your child's good work at sharing.

Activity 2 – Essentials and common property

Like all of us, autistic children prioritise some objects over others. However, autistic children often have a deep connection with one or two particular objects, which may be used for stimming or self-soothing. They may need some of their possessions with them at all times in order to feel safe and supported, but only play with other possessions or people occasionally. Understanding this hierarchy of objects is essential if you want your child to be able to share with other children. They may be very happy to allow another child to play with some of their toys but very threatened if another child wants to play with one of their treasured objects.

Imagine your most prized possession and how you would feel if a family member borrowed that and did not look after it. You may feel anxious or distressed by the possibility of your prized possession being damaged or lost. This anxiety or distress can be hugely magnified for autistic children or young people in relation to their need to look after their most precious possessions. A little bit like you might feel if your car were stolen and you found out it was being used to joy-ride off-road.

Talk to your child about their toys and ascertain the value of them to your child. Ascertain the toys that have special significance to your child and identify those that are less important. After you have categorised the toys, ask your child if they would be happy to share one of the 'lesser' toys with you. Play with the toy and include your child in the game. This may be through talking to your child about what you are doing or getting them to actually interact with the toy at the same time as you. An example of this would be both of you touching a soft toy to move it, one of you holding the toy and the other moving the legs.

Work through different toys to ascertain whether or not your child is happy to play with one or another with you. It is likely there are some toys your child will not want to share. With this exercise, it is actually okay if your child does not end up sharing their precious toys. Sharing these may actually cause them great distress.

Activity 3 – Sharing/playing with other children

Building on Activity 2 above, involve a known child who wants to play with some of your child's toys. Teaching your child to explain that they will not let another child play with their special toy but it is okay to play with one of the toys that is less important to them is a useful lesson. You can do this with all children whether or not they use speech. This is possible because there is a social script for sharing playing, where an early part of the script is around permission to play/share.

You can help your child develop a verbal or action script for sharing toys. This can be done with images, actions and/or words, and essentially means that they can set a limit with other children who might want to play with their most loved and valued toy in a way that still invites sharing/play.

The playing/sharing script:

1. Your child is physically approached by another child who either reaches out for one of their toys or asks – verbally or using Augmentative and Alternative Communication (AAC) – for one of their toys or to play, for example by asking, 'Can I play with your car?'

2. Your child acknowledges the other person with a smile, wave or hello, whilst picking up the item in question.

3. Your child can give the child the item if they are okay with sharing/letting the other child play and either nod, sign or say 'Yes.'

4. If your child does not want the other child to play with that item, they should keep hold of it and shake their head and sign, say or otherwise communicate 'No.'

5. Immediately after a 'no', it is useful to offer an alternate toy for the other child to play with. If your child can pick up and offer a different toy to the child, that can help to build positive interpersonal connections. You may need to model this point a number of times and the communication that goes along with it, by, for example, saying, 'You can play with this instead.' Or, 'I am playing with my blue car, you can play with the red one.' If your child uses a different communication system, you would model using that system, for example by signing or PECS or Prolotogo.

6. Asking for the toy back and/or thanking the child for returning the toy. Again, you will need to model this for your child initially. This step should happen, regardless of whether Step 3 or 4 was used.

Practice the script by acting this out with your child and then by supporting them to do this with well-known children initially. When the opportunity to share arises, parents should observe the beginning of the exchange between their child and another. If you need to step in and intervene because the other child is not responding appropriately and, for example, is snatching your child's favourite toy, you may want to do this. At this point, you may choose to explain the value of that particular toy to your child. However, if you can allow your child to set their own boundaries around sharing/not sharing, this will equip them with a valuable lifelong skill.

Activity 4 – Taking turns with one other person

It can be very difficult to learn turn-taking when you are worried that once it is the other person's turn you will never get another turn! This thinking is related to the autistic 'now is forever' thinking style and the struggles around sequencing and object permanence that many autistics have. This means that teaching resilience around turn-taking and sharing needs to be highly structured to be successful for many autistic children.

One-on-one turn-taking is best taught at home by a parent/carer taking turns explicitly with the child, where the turns start off very short and then over time get longer and less predictable. Some people find the use of visual supports like photos of the child having their turn and waiting and a timer can be helpful.

An example of one-on-one turn-taking would be lining up cars, where each person puts one in the line at a time. When it is your turn, as you pick up the car to place in the line, you say, sign or use a visual to signal 'My turn,' and then once your car is placed, you say, sign or otherwise communicate, 'Your turn.' You may even like to give the child a car to use for their turn.

Other one-on-one turn-taking examples are games like dominos, happy families, snap and snakes and ladders, or activities like turning the page in a book or picking what to watch on TV or what music to listen to. When initially teaching this skill, building in a time/action limit for each person's time is helpful. If you do not do this, the long-term repercussions can be quite profound and annoying for the rest of the family:

My son Tom likes to watch cartoon network on TV, and if we put anything else on, he screams and screams. It is interesting because we always let him decide what we would watch on TV when he was little. But now, it means that we can't ever watch anything we want until he has gone to bed, because if we try, he makes so much noise that we can't hear it. Then, a couple of months ago, he had been staying at my sister's house for a few days, and I went to pick him up, and the news was on TV, and he was sitting in the room quietly looking at a dinosaur book. I couldn't believe it!

My sister is a teacher, and she said she had just been very firm that each person in the house got an allocated time to choose what was on TV, and his time was when he got up in the morning until it was time to get ready for school. After school, it was different people's turns until bedtime. She did admit he had screamed and screamed initially but only on that first day, and that now he could even move the arrow on the little chart she had made of whose turn it was to pick what was on TV.

He told me it would be his turn in the morning again, so he knew he was going to have another turn, and, importantly, the entire house was not being held to ransom by his screaming. So, we decided to do the same thing at home, and he was really, really angry and upset. He said it was always his turn at his house. I thought that my wife and I were just going to have to give in, until I realised that we had never been explicit that it was all of our family's home and we all should get a turn. Yes, he did make a big fuss for about two weeks, but now he is happy with it, as long as no-one touched the TV during his turn. Then it is just awful, but life is so much more enjoyable for the whole family now that we all get to feel equally valuable. (Tom's mother)

Activity 5 – Turn-taking on playground equipment

Many pre-schools and schools allow only one child at a time on the slide or trampoline, so knowing how to take turns on playground equipment is a valuable skill. If your child already has this or is learning this when they start pre-school, it will stand them in good stead and help develop playground resilience. For some children, whether or not they are autistic, watching another child doing something that they are waiting to do is incredibly frustrating. Frustration and autism can be a powerful and unpleasant combination for all concerned!

However, if children understand that they will get a turn and that once their turn is over, it will come around again at some time in the future, they will be more resilient around this turn-taking. Even if your child has developed really good sharing skills with their own toys through the previous exercises and can turn-take with you, it is important to understand that autistic children rarely generalise a skill that they have learnt in one area. This means that they struggle to apply a skill learnt in one area to another area without support.

Turn-taking on playground equipment needs to be introduced in a highly structured and adult-controlled way as playgrounds can look like chaos to many autistic children. You can do this in your own yard or local playground or at kindergarten and so on. You need a second 'skilled' child for this activity as they will be taking turns with your child – this is necessary as many playgrounds do not allow adults on the play equipment.

On your first visit, be prepared just to watch, but also be prepared to go through all the steps! This activity must go at your child's pace and all children are different. This activity may take a lot of practice or be a skill that is picked up very quickly. The only way you will know is by doing and observing. The example given is for a slide and incorporates skill-building supports as well as the key actions. This example activity would need to be replicated with the swings and a trampoline and any other playground equipment that limits the number of people on it to one:

1. Go to the slide with your child, look at the slide and explain the way that people use a slide (schools often do not let children climb up the slide, so explain the safety aspects of different ways of using it). You may want to take photos or a video of your child climbing up the ladder/steps part of the slide and going down the slide part, or your child may just want to watch for a while.

2. You can time approximately how long it takes for someone to go up and down the slide and set up your timer or a visual to help your child know how long their wait time will be. You can also take a turn board with you:

NOW	NEXT	AND THEN

3. Once your child has gone up and down the slide, tell the other child that it is their turn. Make sure your child knows that a turn starts *after* the slide is clear in order to prevent accidental injuries to themselves or others. You may need to communicate 'Wait' to your child, using their preferred form of communication. Remind them that it is their turn soon.

4. As soon as the other child is off the slide, let your child know that it is their turn. If the other child needs reminding, ask them to wait.

5. Repeat steps 2 and 3 until you feel your child will get fed up/ tired soon. At this point, give the other child a prompt that it is their last turn. Tell your child, 'One more turn then we are finished for today.'

6. As your child climbs up, remind them it is the last turn. At the bottom, collect them and talk about when you can next come back to have more turns.

7. Praise the children for waiting for their turn so patiently and for taking turns so well.

Back at home, you can use the photos or video you took to talk through all the above points or to make a new turn-taking board with photos of the children and the actual slide rather than sketches.

Activity 6 – Turn-taking in a group game

Once your child is comfortable taking turns as in Activities 4 and 5, you can build resilience around turn-taking in a group. This is much harder as sometimes the waiting time can be quite significant when compared to the actual doing something time. For this reason, initial experiences with turn-taking in a group should be with activities that are highly motivating where each child has a relatively quick turn and short wait time.

Cooking or baking can be a nice way to introduce group turn-taking skills if your child enjoys these; if not, you may want to use a simple board game or interactive game like pick-up sticks or jenga, where the turn is very visually obvious. Whatever you choose to do, over time, you will need to do a variety of group activities to embed the turn-taking skills in a way that ensures that the child can generalise these to new contexts.

Two examples are given for this activity: snakes and ladders (the board game) and making cookies. Please note that these skills can be learnt by all children, whether or not they use speech. For the cookies, visual recipes can be used along with spoken/written instructions, or the children can even follow along with instructional video clips, with the adult pausing whenever needed. You may choose to use a turn-taking board to let the children know who is doing what when, or you may rely on prompting whose turn it is. A timer is less useful for these activities.

Snakes and ladders

1. Open up the box and ask each of the children to choose an object from the place makers (if you have lost those, buttons or Lego work quite well).

2. Discuss the rules of snakes and ladders, how many dice you will be using, which way round the group turn-taking will go and that you go *up* a ladder and *down* a snake.

3. Talk about when the game ends (when the first person gets to 100).

4. If the adult is playing too, they could either go first to model what to do or last so they are modelling waiting patiently.

5. Start the game. Praise children who wait for their turn patiently.

6. Encourage the children to work out whose turn it is next (children with executive functioning and sequencing difficulties can struggle to do this). Decide if a turn-taking board is needed to support any of the children or not (you can also ask them if they would want one).

Making cookies

You can use a box of pre-mix for this or use your own recipe. Whichever you do, make sure you have a large written and/or pictorial/video version for the children to follow. Young children find measuring using cups and spoons easier than reading scales. Children with severe food allergies to nuts, eggs, wheat and/or milk should not touch these ingredients or surfaces that have been in contact with these items, so pick your recipe and ingredients to suit your particular group.

Ensure that all children wash their hands and, if using water instead of alcohol rub, that they dry their hands, too. Children can either share one large bowl and collectively make the cookie dough and then get a share of it to make their 'own' cookies, or they can take turns throughout the whole process. Children should be around a table, with a clear line of sight to the ingredients and the equipment.

Each child should get an opportunity to add ingredients and stir, as well as roll out dough, cut and, if decorating, decorate. Some children do not like to stop stirring and hand the bowl on, so the adult needs to remind them to pass it on to the next child for their turn and praise their excellent stirring skills. Having a pictorial recipe there helps to demonstrate that the children will all be getting more turns to do things, right up to putting the cookies on the tray and washing everything up:

> When I had been teaching for a few years, I used to make bread with my class every week. The children took turns measuring and stirring in small groups and then they each got some dough to knead and make into bread-roll shapes to go in the oven. Over a term, they all developed the skills to wait or request someone give them their turn, and I got to eat a lot of yummy bread! Ever since, I have been a great fan of cooking with children and spent a while in a special school creating a picture recipe for each week, so that the recipes were accessible to all the students. (Emma)

TRAVELLING LONG DISTANCE

> When I was a child, we had to travel long distance. There was no music, certainly no DVD screens for the backseat passengers. There were no iPads, laptops or mobile phones. Long car journeys usually involved my brother and I talking civilly for about 20 km and then being a little rude to one another and then spending the rest of the trip trying to kill each other! The entertainment we had was games like '20 questions' or 'I spy'. It was pretty dire. (Ben)

Ben's story demonstrates the challenges of long-distance travel in the past, but even in this day and age, long-distance travel can be challenging for autistic children for a number of different reasons. Long-distance car trips can be difficult due to the sensory issues involved, for a start. Heat from the sunshine, the feeling of the motion of the car and the sights of the world whizzing past outside the window can be overwhelming for some people. It should be noted that there are also some autistics who love sitting in cars, or as adults driving, precisely because of the sensory input.

A car is an enclosed space in which you are effectively trapped whilst it is moving. Parents or other adults usually decide which route to take and where and when to stop. This means that car journeys can become an unknown quantity and something beyond the child's control. If the journey is to a new place or a place that the child has been before and found unpleasant in the past, this can impact negatively on the child's sense of their place of safety. Some children are anxious in cars or experience motion sickness, which can also increase anxiety. In addition, because the now can feel like forever to some autistics, the child may be feeling as if they will be trapped in the car forever and are never going to be able to get out and do what they want to do.

Trips overseas can be extremely challenging. They may involve getting up early in the morning to go to the airport. Some autistic children love aeroplanes but some don't. A child not doing well on an international flight will almost certainly draw negative attention from other passengers and, at times, flight crew, which may well be picked up on by the child, increasing their anxiety and potentially making things worse. You may choose to request assistance from the airline and request boarding last or first, whichever suits your child best. Some airlines are more accommodating than others on this.

Small children may not understand the concept of other countries and may worry about where they are going. In a different country, people may speak a different language, cities and landscapes might seem very foreign, the food might be different and it may be impossible to get the food the child normally eats. What is a great holiday for parents and older siblings can be a nightmare for a young autistic child. On the other hand, some autistic children and adults love foreign and/or long-distance travel and continue to engage in this as much as possible throughout life.

As with many other challenging situations, the key to building resilience and mastery with long-distance travel is preparation, both of your child and of yourselves. If your child has some idea of what to expect, the experience is less likely to be traumatic and may even be highly enjoyable. Plan to have some of your child's preferred possessions and food available if you are able. Tell them as much as you can about what the journey and destination are likely to be like.

Ensure that you have activities and food/drink accessible to the child during long-distance travel, and make sure that you have planned for toilet time and access! If your child likes to wear headphones, noise-cancelling headphones can be the difference between a child liking being on a plane or in a crowded noisy environment and not being able to tolerate it. It is also important to note that things your child likes normally may be too much for them to manage after a long journey:

> I quite like music and go to concerts a couple of times a year. The excitement and sensory input of the music is usually enough to mitigate my sensory dislike of crowds. However, I went to one concert after a really long day at work involving five hours of driving. I had to leave before the second song had finished, as I just couldn't cope with the reverb, and I had used up all my mental energy in the car throughout the day. I also can't function as well if I do a business trip that involves two flights in one day, not sure why, things just seem to get so much harder then. It is the same with plane travel; I need a day to recover. (Emma)

Some indicators that your child is managing well with long-distance and/or overseas travel are:

- Decreasing levels of distress/meltdowns when your child has to travel long distance.

- Your child takes an interest in the destination or responds in a neutral or positive manner to discussion of long-distance travel.

- Your child asks questions about a planned trip.

- Your child starts to build some self-soothing strategies for long-distance trips (e.g. asks for their favourite book or DVD on each car trip).

Activity 1 – Incremental journeys

This activity involves gradually increasing your child's tolerance for long trips by taking incrementally longer trips. Reinforce success when they master a longer trip and focus on how well they are mastering the challenge. If they have a setback, try to work out what the issue was – sometimes your child will be able to articulate this on some level and sometimes they won't. Do not give up on introducing long-distance travel for your child and encourage them for the next time rather than berating them for not achieving the goal. You can do both car/bus journeys as well as journeys on foot.

This means that you may start off walking to the postbox together, and then walking to the next house down, and then around the block, and so on. If you are increasing bus or car trips, it is important to remember that, although your child needs to know where they are going, you do not want to make them dependent on following 'the one and only correct route' to go somewhere. This means that you may go left one day and right the next and then straight on, on another day. You can have a map in the car or with you on the bus so you can help your child know where they are in relation to other people/places at all times:

> We used to live in Christchurch in New Zealand, the earthquake city. It was problematic for many autistics, both adults and children after the earthquakes. If they only knew one right way to get somewhere, they physically couldn't go that way anymore because the road didn't exist anymore. For families, like ours, where kids had lots of meltdowns around it, it was really stressful, but for autistics who couldn't work out what to do to get where they needed to go, it was horrendous. The experience really made me understand why we need to teach our autistic children a variety of ways to do things and get places. (Tom)

Activity 2 – Planning trips together

If you have a long trip planned, work with your child to plan the journey. This planning should include activities for the journey as well as an idea of what to expect and what they might do when they arrive at their destination. If there is an attraction in the place where you are going that relates to your child's interest or passion, do some research about this and relate what you discover to your child. It is likely they will be excited about going once they know there is an attraction they want to see. Wanting to do an activity can be a great motivator for your child to go through all the steps it takes to get there.

If you are planning to do or see a particular thing, it is important to check whether or not it will be open and whether or not you and/or your child will have access to it. There is a lot of disappointment waiting to be unpleasantly expressed in situations where an autistic is not able to do or see something that they have just spent hours or even days/weeks/months planning to see!

If your child has their own travel bags, they can pack these by themselves (with supervision so as to ensure you do not break any laws accidentally). If not, they can help check off lists of what needs packing/ has been packed in the family bags.

When explaining how long it will take to get to somewhere, factor in things that can go wrong! This is being typed on a flight to Darwin that should have landed over an hour ago... Long-distance travel can bring out the worst in many people, so preparation for a range of contingencies can be helpful to support resilience for travel.

Activity 3 – Focus on positives

Many parents when confronted with the need to travel long distances with a young child – and particularly a young child on the autism spectrum who may have challenges with holding attention, sensory issues and new environments – will be anxious and focus on damage control rather than enjoying their trip. The anxiety or stress that the adult is experiencing can often be picked up on by the autistic child and increase their anxiety and distress. However, with good preparation as discussed in Activity 2, this anxiety/stress should be contained.

This activity involves the parent trying to approach the experience of travel differently. When you speak with your child about the trip, be excited and interested. Focus on the positives with your child such as talking to them about going on an aeroplane for the first time (or again) and all the good things that might involve. Your attitude about something may be picked up on by your child, meaning if you are anxious and negative about a trip that will carry through in your conversations. Of course, travel can involve a lot of stressful things so prepare for those, but in your conversations with your child try to focus on the positives and the interesting activities they can do.

Whenever I fly through turbulence, I think about one of my friends, who loves turbulence as it is aerodynamics in action. Sometimes, the science/facts behind experiences can really grab the attention and interest of autistic children and shift their focus from anxiety to interest and excitement. You can also tailor your discussions to support a focus on your child's passion. If your child likes clouds, they could draw all the different kinds of clouds they see from the plane during the trip (if they sit where they can see out of the window). If they love cars, they can tally the different colours, sizes, types of cars on the freeway and so on.

Activity 4 – The travel 'road map'

You can make a story, video or drawing with your child to help them understand what the travel and the destination will be like. For autistic children – and adults, too – uncertainty about an activity can be more anxiety-provoking than the activity itself. They may be worried that they don't know what the trip will involve, what the location will look like and who will be there. A good thing to do is create in your child's mind a 'road map' or image of what each stage of the travel will be like.

Dependent on your child's approach and interests, you can work through different elements of the travel. If they like building and mapping games like Minecraft, that might be a good way to explain the travel and help to give them their mental road map to lessen anxiety for the trip. If they are more interested in art, you can work with them on a poster with the elements of the upcoming trip. You can use photos of relatives they may not have met or pictures of the location.

You can also use a real map, whether a paper or electronic version. It is really easy now to create a map that shows the whole journey, no matter what form of transportation is being used. You can print or photocopy these so that your child has a copy with them for the journey as well as to look at during journey preparations.

MEETING A NEW PET

Meeting a new pet should be a happy occasion, and it often is. However, some autistic children can struggle with the change to routine brought about by a new furry, feathered or scaly addition to the house. Other difficulties can arise if the pet is not quite what the child expected, either in terms of the way it looks or sounds or feels, or what it does. It is important to research your pet options realistically, giving your child clear information about things like the smell of puppy poo if you are planning to bring a puppy into your home.

Many autistic people have a strong affinity with animals, which seems to begin very early in their life. Many autistic adults remember always having loved cats, dogs or guinea pigs (or whatever else). Autistic children in a family with no pets may become very persuasive in asking their parent/s to get them whichever animal it is they feel an affinity for. When this happens, a flat-out 'no' is rarely effective at stopping the requests. Instead, look into the animal with your child and work through all the impacts of that animal on the household, including financial and time costs, and the physical needs of the animal:

> I really wanted my own pet. We had dogs, but I refused to help look after them, because my mum bought them, and I felt that they were her responsibility not mine. I got some chickens and was happy to collect the eggs, feed them and clean their hen house. What I really loved to do, though, was pick up the chickens and talk to them. I loved the feel of their feathers when I petted them and they were wonderful to just be with. But when we moved into the city, we had to leave them for the next people in the house. It would have been cruel to have the chickens in a tiny yard with no room to roam and scratch. (Robbie)

Pets can be a great addition to the household for a number of reasons. They can help children learn how to be responsible, gentle and considerate. Pets have considerable health and well-being benefits for autistic children, too. Some autistic people are closer to their pet than they are to anyone or anything else. A pet can be a friend, confidant, companion and supporter for an autistic child.

As mentioned, some of the challenges around pet ownership include the pet not meeting the child's expectations. For instance, a young child may love cats and have persistently lobbied their parent for a kitten of their own, expecting the cat to want cuddles all the time. Where children have formed an attachment to an animal from information that is only second-hand, such as the TV, books or the internet, it is important that they get all the information to round out their initial impressions, before the pet is acquired. Many real cats are not overly affectionate or only want affection occasionally, whereas many internet cats appear to be quite interactive and amusing. Another potential challenge with pet ownership is the more onerous jobs associated with looking after pets – cleaning cages and hutches, emptying cat litter or picking up after a dog.

A new pet can also play havoc with the household routine. A new puppy might bark or cry all night, fretting for his mother. A cat may meow or scratch at the door, impacting on sleep. The routine which dictates the exact time that breakfast is taken may change if a dog needs a walk or the toilet. These things can be challenging. A useful strategy is to focus on the positives around pet ownership and why the child wanted the pet in the first place. It can also help to let your child know that changes in sleep or routine caused by a new pet are often transitory and will resolve in time. Using your child's natural sense of justice and interest in the animal, you can help your child learn to compromise on their routines in order to best care for their pet.

Preferred outcomes: That your child accepts the pet and develops a positive caring relationship with the pet.

Some indicators that your child is adapting well to the addition of a new pet include:

- They evidently love the pet – initiating play, giving affection and so forth.

- The pet finds his or her way into your child's play/imaginary world and drawings as a positive character.

- Your child manages changes in routine well – they have a lower level of distress and difficult behaviour.

ACTIVITIES AROUND WELCOMING A NEW PET

Many autistic children respond well to animals and have a strong affinity with cats or dogs or lizards and so on. However, some autistic children are very anxious around animals. In rare instances, children may be aggressive towards pets, either deliberately or by giving affection that is unintentionally rough or frightening for the pet. Where children are unaware of how firmly they touch other people, it is important to teach them how to interact safely with animals before they are left alone with them.

Activity 1 – The role play pet

When preparing to adopt a new pet, your child may be anxious or frightened of the possibility of the pet. If they are not anxious, they may have the opposite problem in that they are too confident and hands-on. Many pets do not respond well to unwanted affection given many times a day from an overly enthusiastic child.

One activity that may help is getting your child a stuffed toy that is a cat or dog or whatever pet you intend to adopt. Explain to your child that the stuffed animal is quite like the animal you will be getting. Treat the stuffed toy as you would the new pet and explain to your child how to look after the pet and be gentle and attend to the real pet's needs of food, water, shelter and so on. Encourage your child to bond with their 'pet' – give it a name and play with it. When you adopt the real-life pet, you can even give it the same or a similar name to the stuffed toy. Some children do not respond to soft toys but if your child does, this can be a very helpful way of preparing them for a real pet. You can even buy some robot 'pets' that are quite lifelike and respond to touch and sound:

JENNY'S STORY

When I was about 9, I had a cat. I had wanted a cat for as long as I could remember. I was so excited when my mum came home with Shadow – a little black kitten. I loved Shadow so much, but I didn't know how to show my love in a way that didn't actually upset the cat. I tried to cuddle Shadow all the time, and she wasn't a very cuddly cat anyway. One day, my mum saw me chase Shadow under a chair. My mum asked me if I would like a big person chasing after me and trying to cuddle me all the time. At first I thought the image of a big person chasing me around was silly, but eventually I worked out what my mum meant and was gentler with Shadow. I figured I wouldn't like a giant chasing me around and always wanting cuddles!

Activity 2 – Part of the family

Some autistic children struggle to connect with a pet, or if they do connect, they don't have a good understanding of how rough handling might cause anxiety in their pet. This can stem from them seeing pets as different to the human inhabitants of the house. Of course, pets *are* different but they still need love and respect.

For this activity, show your child videos or books looking at how best to handle and treat the kind of animal you will be getting. Talk about the pet being a family member like the parent(s), child, his or her siblings and extended family are. Talk through how your child likes people to treat them and explain that the pet will have the same sorts of feelings as your child does – even if it has fur and can't explain in English that it doesn't like something or is scared. Helping the child explore how different touch feels on their own arm can help them to learn the concept of gentle hands.

Walk around the house with your child and identify where the pet might live or have its bed, food, water and so on. Together, work out areas that are just for the pet, so the pet can have alone time. This is not necessary for fish!

Activity 3 – Meet other pets

When you are planning to bring a new pet into the household, you can take your child to meet other pets owned by friends and family members. Explain the pet's actions to your child (e.g. 'Miss Kitty is licking her paws, because that is how cats clean themselves and cats like to be clean'). Allow your child to watch and interact with the pet at their own pace, unless their actions might antagonise the pet and cause aggression. In that case, use your 'No!'

If your child is anxious around animals, support them to get to know the pets they visit better without forcing close contact. For a child who is anxious around animals, this might take some time but, providing no difficulties occur, such as aggression from the pet, they should be able to build their confidence around pets to a point that having one at home is enjoyable and rewarding and not frightening.

If you are unable to have a mammal in your home because you rent your home, you could look at other animals such as lizards or stick insects. Many autistic adults who have these kinds of pets recall with great happiness when they got their first reptile or insect. Other options are to share a pet with another family, where you and your child can help look after the animal but it lives with the other family. In Japan, they even have cat cafés, so people can pet and feed cats!

Activity 4 – Introducing responsibility

With older children, having pets can be a great opportunity to build their level of responsibility through giving them tasks around feeding and looking after pets. With younger children, there is also an opportunity for them to gain some responsibility.

This activity involves giving your child small regular tasks around looking after the pet. It could be that they fill the water bowl or even that they give the pet a gentle cuddle. When they do this, give positive feedback and encouragement around how responsible they have been. Make responsibility for looking after pets an enjoyable experience. If your child is very good at this activity, you could introduce slightly greater levels of responsibility for pet care.

Taking on responsibility is a great skill related to resilience and independence. Pets can have the added bonus that autistic children may bond strongly and the pet will become an additional support for your child. In addition, many autistic children struggle to develop awareness of thirst and hunger and the understanding of the need to eat healthily and drink water regularly in order to optimise their own development. By learning how to look after their pet's needs, they can learn about the role of food/nutrition and water in an age-appropriate but relevant and meaningful way. For example, you might say 'Look, Scruffy's water bowl is empty. Scruffy will get thirsty. Let's fill up the water so Scruffy can have a drink. Dogs need water to be healthy, just like people do.'

GOING TO THE DOCTOR'S/HOSPITAL

Some children love going to the doctor, however, for the first or subsequent few visits, it can be very challenging for some autistic children. The doctor might perform some examinations that involve physical contact or invasive procedures. If the autistic child is not prepared for this, it can induce meltdowns and distress. In addition, health professionals do not always use autistic communication styles when interacting and can give misleading information that can cause long-term distress in relation to going to the doctor or nurse. An example of this is when children have vaccines or have blood taken and the health professional says that it won't hurt. A more honest and autistic style of communicating would be to say, 'This will hurt briefly, but as soon as it is over, it will stop hurting. The little hurt is to help your body be stronger to help you stay well and not be very sick.'

The waiting room might cause sensory overload. The wait is often quite long and some good GPs are always running behind schedule due to high demand for their services and their attention to their patients. If you take your child to the emergency department, the wait may be for several hours if the condition for which you are seeking treatment is not life-threatening. Hospital emergency department waiting rooms can be hell for autistic kids and their parents. A combination of long waits with no known end point, sensory issues and unexpected actions of hospital staff and being in a room full of sick people can be a nightmare for autistic children.

When you actually get to talk with the doctor, they may be more or less understanding around autism. Some doctors are knowledgeable and supportive, but others can be dismissive and blame parents for their child's apparent 'naughty' behaviour. Many autistic children benefit from the doctor explaining what they are going to do and why. The doctor just shoving a cold stethoscope firmly onto a child's chest may cause extreme anxiety and fear. You can ask the doctor to explain clearly to your child what they're going to do before they do it.

EXERCISE: UNDERSTANDING AUTISTIC——————————
CHILDREN'S PERSPECTIVES

Imagine you are a 5-year-old autistic child going to the doctor's clinic. You have never been to this place before. It smells funny and there are lots of old people, some of whom want to talk to you for some reason. You are in a room with the term 'Waiting Room' on the door.

How long is the waiting going to be for if there is a whole room for waiting! People come out of doors and call names and people waiting follow them into a room with a closed door. Why is the door closed? What is going to happen in there? You are frightened. Eventually your name is called. You don't want to go but your mum really seems to want you to go in. You get into the room and there is an older man who smells strongly of cologne. It is overwhelming, and you go to leave but your mum ushers you back to sit next to her. The strong-smelling man is talking to your mum. You can't work out what they are saying. You are bored, but there is nothing to play with in this room. You start using the desk as a drum. It makes you feel good, and you get lost in the rhythm. The smelly man suddenly says your name and asks you to open your mouth. 'Why?' you think. You think he's going to put some yucky food in your mouth, so you keep it closed. It is evident from how your mum and the smelly man react that you are doing something wrong. You don't understand this. You are trying to defend yourself from a man you have never met before who wants to do things to you for some mysterious reason that hasn't really been explained to you.

You start getting really stressed and start drumming again as it makes you feel calmer. Both the man and your mum tell you to stop doing this, so you do, but you are still really stressed. The man puts his hand on your shoulder. This is just simply too much on top of everything else. You have a huge meltdown, which you get punished for. You hope you don't ever have to come to this place again.

A large number of autistic children have medical issues, such as gastrointestinal issues, seizure disorders, autoimmune issues and/or developmental difficulties such as Down's syndrome or ADHD. It is not known why this is, but as a result many autistic children need to visit the doctor and/or hospital, in addition to well child checks and so on:

My youngest child has had a number of big seizures; she also has some other medical issues. She became really frightened of doctors and hospitals, and that was problematic, because she needs to go there for treatment when she is sick. Once we started advocating for her and getting a reduced sensory environment, less noise, less lights, and telling the staff how to talk to her, to be honest, things improved. She still doesn't like it, but it is not as distressing as it was. (Michelle)

Preferred outcomes: Learning how to manage at the doctor's surgery or emergency room is likely to be a more incremental process, given the large number of potential stressors that exist in these settings, particularly if your child has had a painful or stressful experience already. What you would like is for them to be able and willing to seek medical assistance when required.

Some indicators that your child is doing well with managing seeing the doctor include:

- Decreasing overload, distress and meltdowns in medical settings or when your child is told that they have to see the doctor.

- Learning effective self-soothing strategies (stimming, fidget toy, etc.).

- Low or no refusal to attend medical appointments.

- A greater understanding of the reasons they may need to visit the doctor.

ACTIVITIES AROUND GOING TO THE DOCTOR
Activity 1 – Role playing – seeing the doctor

One of the scariest things for autistic children going to the doctor is physical contact that is, or is perceived as invasive. Some children are really sensitive and can respond with meltdown or shutdown when a health professional touches their body or takes their temperature. One of the issues can be that this activity is unfamiliar as the child has never had it happen before. Another reason is that they do not understand what is happening, as demonstrated in the exercise described at the start of this section.

You can help prepare your child for visits to the doctor by showing your child the sorts of things a doctor would do and then role playing things like asking them to open their mouth, taking their temperature or feeling their abdomen. A good way to do this is to start the exercise by role playing these activities with a doll or soft toy. Then, once your child has some idea of what happens, you can get your child to do the pretend medical examinations on you. Model the sort of response you want your child to give when they go to the doctor. You can express fun or amusement to make the process seem less scary and unpleasant. Once your child has been the 'doctor', ask if you can be *their* doctor. Then practise what a GP might do with your child. Be conscious of whether this is causing distress and, if it is, maybe leave it there for the moment but revisit it later. You may also choose to use video modelling to enable your child to see a real GP visit. This would need the consent of the GP involved.

Activity 2 – Visiting the hospital

If you know that your child has a hospital appointment coming up, it is better to visit the hospital beforehand so that they can see where they will be going, without the stress of the appointment. If this is not possible because you live a long way away, have a look at photos of the hospital on their website.

If you do go and visit, you can video your child going into and coming out of the hospital and play this for them before they go for this appointment. This will help them to understand that they are not going to stay in the hospital forever. Some hospitals will let autistic children visit the specialist's room prior to the appointment, whilst others do not have the ability to do this because of pressure on clinical time and/or space.

Activity 3 – Making a health passport with your child

It can help your child to have their own 'health passport' which they create with you. This can have as little or as much information as you both want. It should have your child's name and they can draw a picture of themselves and something they like. Whenever your child goes to the doctor or hospital, you can put a stamp or sticker in their health passport. As they get older, their passport can be renewed, so that it stays age and stage appropriate.

GOING TO THE DENTIST

For autistic children, and many autistic adults, visiting the dentist is incredibly stressful. It essentially involves a stranger putting their finger in children's mouths and then putting strange metal instruments in there. There are some very unusual smells and sounds, which for somebody who has sensitivities around smell and/or sounds can be overwhelming. The process is anxiety-provoking and much of the worry is the anticipation. If a child has a bad experience at the dentist the first time they go, it can set up a whole load of anxiety, which makes it extremely difficult or impossible for the child to return. Some dentists and their staff members are aware of the needs of autistic kids, but many aren't. If a child has a meltdown in the dentist's surgery, their parent can be subjected to misplaced statements on discipline and judgement, compounding the issues even further.

Another concern around dental care is that for many autistic children, the taste of toothpaste or the sensation of a toothbrush in their mouth is extremely unpleasant and triggers negative sensory responses. This means that the child may need to visit the dentist even more frequently, leading to further anxiety and overload. This, in turn, can lead to children simply never going to the dentist and flatly refusing to go. It can also mean a lifetime of poor oral hygiene and all the issues that come with that.

Explicitly teaching *why* children should clean their teeth is a helpful first step as this in conjunction with a healthy diet will minimise the need for dental visits. However, being able to visit the dentist and get a check-up or work done is an important skill, particularly for children. Medical and dental experiences and anxiety around them can keep autistic adults from getting necessary dental or medical work done, leading to pain and discomfort, which can sometimes escalate to a dangerous situation, such as a dental abscess that needs urgent attention.

One of the difficulties with autistic children and the dentist is that the first visit sets up a negative expectation and anxiety around dental visits in your child's mind. Another issue is if a child does not understand what the dentist is doing or why they are doing it, the whole thing can just seem like deliberate and unnecessary torture by a scary adult in a white jacket wearing rubber gloves:

When I was a child, I lived in the UK. At the time, they had free public dental care, so when we were quite young my brother and I started going to the dentist for check-ups. It was always made into a fun game by my mum. When we sat in the chair and it moved, it was the most exciting thing in the world! My brother and I called the dentist the 'bentist', because he bent kids into funny shapes with his chair. When he called out to his nurse 'Erupting!' meaning an adult tooth was coming in, my brother and I thought this was hilarious, like there was a volcano in our mouth! There was never any suggestion of the need to be scared of the dentist. I didn't even realise people were scared of the dentist until one of my classmates said she was. I am so grateful to my mum for making it a game as it meant I am able to go to the dentist now without a lot of anxiety. (Jenny)

It should be noted that some autistic children are so anxious about dental work that they need it to be done under full sedation. Your child certainly hasn't 'failed' if that is them and their anxiety isn't 'weakness'. However, it is better not to pursue this as the first option: first, because it is costly; but, second, because if your child is in an accident or has a life-threatening illness, the ability to sit through unpleasant and invasive medical procedures is a very good protective factor to ensure that they can manage interventions for life-threatening medical interventions.

Signs that your child is managing going to the dentist well include:

- They are able to go to the appointment and get through the examination.

- They are not overwhelmed with anxiety and fear about going to the dentist.

- They show an interest in looking after their teeth.

- Meltdowns/shutdowns in relation to dental appointments either don't happen or are reducing in frequency and intensity.

ACTIVITIES TO BUILD RESILIENCE AROUND DENTAL CARE

Activity 1 – Preparation

Try to ensure that your child's first experience of going to the dentist is not entirely negative and scary. It might be worth asking around with other parents you know as to which are the best dentists in your area for autistic kids. Some dentists are excellent, while others have very little idea about the way an autistic child experiences the dentist's office. Talk to your child about their teeth and why it is important to look after them. If your child is sensitive to toothpaste or the sensation of brushing, look into alternatives. There are some three-sided, soft toothbrushes created with autistic kids in mind that many find helpful. Tell your child about your teeth and when you have needed to go to the dentist yourself. Explain that it can be uncomfortable but it is necessary.

Activity 2 – Going to the dentist

Before your child's first visit to the dentist, call the dental clinic and ask if it is okay to bring your child in for a practice visit. If the dentist who your child will be seeing is amenable to it, introduce your child to the dentist and have them explain their job. Some children will find elements of the dentist's clinic fun – like the chair. Ask the dentist if your child can 'have a go' in the dentist chair if they are interested in doing so. If the dentist is amenable, he or she can talk to your child about the sort of things which happen at the dentist. You can make some Social Stories™ or role plays about the dentist, too. Ask if you can record the sounds of the teeth cleaning implements and then listen to these at home – your child can then decide if they can tolerate the sound or if they would prefer to wear headphones during their visit.

Activity 3 – A dental check-up

When the day comes for your child's first visit, stay with them while the dentist is looking at their teeth. Ask the dentist to tell your child all the things he or she is doing and why, and reassure your child that the dentist won't be doing what they are doing for long. Make sure that you or the dentist explains to your child that if they feel pain, discomfort or are scared, they can raise their hand and the dentist will stop what they are doing but they may need to restart a little later. When the appointment is finished, ask if your child wants to ask the dentist any questions about what they did. Give your child a reward.

LEARNING NEW MOTOR SKILLS – PUTTING ON CLOTHES AND SHOES

Many autistic children have difficulties with executive functioning like sequencing as well as difficulties with gross and fine motor skills, so learning new skills like putting on socks and shoes, doing up a zipper, fastening buttons and pulling on a t-shirt can be incredibly challenging.

Coupled with the tendency for autistic children to struggle with new skills, and the need to explicitly learn each new step, you can end up with a very frustrated and stressed child, who wants to be able to do up buttons right now but hasn't yet acquired the skill. Some parents might compare their autistic child's performance at dressing with a sibling, cousin or other child of a similar age. This approach can in fact have the perverse consequence of the child becoming more anxious around dressing themselves and that anxiety meaning they are less physically able to do the task at hand.

If a child is still struggling with buttons and zippers when they reach school age, things like going to the toilet can be difficult. The child may require assistance from the teacher, which could lead to social embarrassment and feelings of shame, if it is not managed with sensitivity. It is apparent that being able to dress oneself is a highly useful skill for a number of reasons – some of which are intangible and relate to the child's sense of self-identity and self-worth.

Different children will learn to get dressed and put on shoes at different ages. There is a good range of clothes and shoes for children that are easier to put on – for example, shoes that fasten using Velcro instead of laces or buckles. Some autistic children have significant negative sensory experiences with clothes and shoes. The sounds of Velcro being torn open can be a horrific auditory experience for some autistic children. These sensory issues can have an impact on a child's willingness and capacity to be able to dress themselves and put on shoes. Shirts may feel horribly itchy or tags on clothes may cause unbearable irritation. If your child refuses to wear something, don't force them to wear it. If you can, ask them what the problem is with the garment and be guided by their concerns.

There are a few simple strategies that can help your child to wear clothes with reduced sensory discomfort, such as wearing seamless socks, bamboo-fibre clothes (which are softer than cotton and other fibres), turning socks inside out or wearing shirts with the label printed on the fabric not as a separate tag. If your child particularly likes a certain item or brand of clothing, it can be helpful to buy a number of them and buy it in larger sizes. Some commentators claim, such strategies are 'a cop-out'. However, these strategies are readily available, and there is no reason a child needs to do up shoelaces or buttons when they are small if doing so causes high anxiety. It seems common sense to use strategies to address that anxiety. There is no deadline for these things and fastening buttons and tying shoelaces are motor skills that can be acquired at a later age.

Preferred outcomes: That your child is willing and able to wear shoes and clothing appropriately.

There are some indicators that your child is doing well with dressing themselves:

- They are able to dress themselves and put on shoes with less or no assistance.

- They are able to communicate sensory issues with clothes to a parent.

- There is decreasing or no distress getting dressed or putting on shoes.

- The amount of time it takes your child to get ready and leave the house decreases.

ACTIVITIES AROUND PUTTING ON CLOTHES AND SHOES

Motor skills are a difficult area to apply activities to make the child more proficient, as many autistic children and adults will struggle to acquire some aspects of motor skills. As such, activities around motor skills need to focus on supporting your child to do the best they can with the motor skills they have and to increase these incrementally, rather than to place an unrealistic goal that will probably result in frustrations and feelings of failure and inadequacy.

With things like putting on shoes and clothes, a good activity is to work out with your child what sorts of fasteners are best for them. Try not to make this a punitive or negative experience based on the idea that your child is deficient for not being able to tie laces. Carrying out the task of finding shoes and clothes that your child can put on and including them in the decision is much more likely to build their resilience and confidence.

Activity 1 – Finding things to help

This activity involves supporting your child to identify strategies that work for them. In the context of motor skills and putting on shoes and clothes, it is important to remember that there are two components to dressing – getting things on and fastening them. Support your child to work out which things are easiest to put on/preferred, which fastenings they can manage independently and which still need support. You can use Montessori dressing frames or make your own, or use baby clothes on a large doll or teddy to model how to open and close the various types of fasteners.

If your child cringes or melts down at particular sounds of certain fastenings, such as Velcro, then you know to avoid that for now.

By practising doing up things in this way, you can identify which types of clothing are going to help your child be independent in their dressing and what still needs to be taught. Shoe laces can be taught in stages or you can buy no-tie laces. Many adults wear slip-on shoes and these no longer have any negative connotations and are quite normal and acceptable in schools. This identification of strategies and tweaks to make life easier to navigate, combined with your child having agency through making a decision or observation around what works for them, is an important step in building independence and resilience.

Activity 2 – Sequencing dressing

Many autistic children struggle to learn dressing sequences and will sometimes put clothes on top of their pyjamas or put their shoes on before their socks and so on. Other autistics struggle to remember which way round shirts go and can go out in clothes that are inside out or back to front. All of these can be very frustrating for autistic children, especially when other people tease them or make mean comments about their dressing skills or how they are wearing their clothes.

In this activity, you take a photo of (or draw) your child, with each item being put on in sequence. So, picture one might be in their underwear, picture two with underwear and socks, picture three underwear, socks and t-shirt, picture four adds in pants/shorts and picture five adds shoes, and so on. You can then use these to make a visual schedule for your child so that they know what to put on and in what order.

Some children prefer video self-modelling, where instead of a photo visual schedule, you record a video of them getting dressed correctly and they can play this for themselves on an iPad/tablet/phone in the morning before getting dressed.

Activity 3 – Discovering sensory issues with clothing

A significant issue for many autistic children around clothing and footwear is sensory (tactile) issues. Things like tags or certain fibres in cloth can be unbearable. So, your child complaining bitterly about getting dressed may, in fact, be because their shirt feels like sandpaper and the thought of wearing it all day is almost unbearable. Or, it may be that they get very hot in some fabrics and so refuse to wear those fabrics.

Sensory issues experienced by autistic people are not always well understood. If you are unsure about your child's sensory experiences, you can do this activity, which involves having your child wear some of their everyday clothes. While they are wearing the clothes, ask them what it feels like on their skin – if it is nice or not nice. If they can't articulate how the clothes feel, ask them another question: 'Does it feel good or does it feel bad?' or 'Do you like wearing this or not?'

There are lots of different fabrics that are sensory friendly. Many people with sensory sensitivities prefer bamboo-fibre clothes. Shirts with the tag printed on the fabric rather than as a label are also preferred by many. Sensory sensitivities can have a huge impact on a child's behaviour and sense of well-being so it is important to know if this is an issue (Goodall 2013). Taking your child to a fabric store or clothing shop simply to feel the fabrics while you take note of their reactions can be very helpful in working out sensory issues with fabrics. In addition, washing clothes repeatedly or with particular fabric conditioners can make some fabrics more acceptable to some autistic children. In contrast, some prefer crisp, ironed fabrics:

I had never worn wool until I was about 8, and I couldn't believe everyone else was happily wearing this awful stuff that made me itch and my skin feel all agitated. I made such a fuss that the school gave me a different costume to wear in the class play! To this day, I can't wear anything wool touching my skin. (Lila)

REFERENCES

Goodall, E. (2013) *Understanding and Facilitating the Achievement of Autistic Potential.* CreateSpace Independent Publishing Platform.

Harpster, K., Burkett, K., Walton, K. and Case-Smith, J. (2015) 'Evaluating the effects of the engagement–communication–exploration (ECE) snack time intervention for preschool children with autism spectrum disorder (ASD).' *American Journal of Occupational Therapy 69* (Supplement1), 6911515227p1-6911515227p1.

Nederkoorn, C., Jansen, A. and Havermans, R.C. (2015) 'Feel your food: The influence of tactile sensitivity on picky eating in children.' *Appetite 84,* 7–10. Available at www.unisa.edu.au/Global/Health/Sansom/Documents/iCAHE/DECD%20journal%20club%20page/Feel%20your%20food_2015.pdf (accessed 20 December 2016).

COMMON ISSUES FOR AUTISTIC CHILDREN AND THEIR FAMILIES BETWEEN AGES SEVEN AND TEN

INTRODUCTION

As children start to grow older, much of their time is spent at school, and it becomes more likely that they and you will face challenges to resilience. Primary school years can be fantastic for some autistic children and very challenging for others. Questions around communication used and capability of your autistic child may seem to occur more or less frequently than you or they would like. Most autistic children, whether or not they have a diagnosis, have a sense of being different in school. Many also start to build a sense of identity based on the way that other people interact with and talk about them. This makes it critical that they have positive interactions with peers and adults around them. In addition, it becomes more important than ever not to talk about your autistic child negatively in their hearing, which can be a lot more acute than you realise. When someone says something negative to you about your autistic child, it can help your child to understand how much you value them if you respond with something positive about your child.

All children have strengths and support needs. Helping your child to understand that and to be aware of their own strengths and support needs can significantly impact on their sense of self, and build resilience around requiring support and the ways that various people respond to that. When children feel that they are less able than everyone around, it can make life quite difficult for them, emotionally, socially and in terms of moving forward to achieve their potential.

This does not mean that you should not discuss when your child has done something that hurt or upset others, but that you should frame these as learning points and not an inherent flaw in your child. Autistic children are very concrete in their thinking, for example they often assume that 'now is forever' and that when someone thinks less of them, they will always think less of them. This can also lead autistic children to assume that if someone is angry with them, they will always be angry with them. This makes open, honest and clear communication very important. You need to help your child understand that you are angry about what happened, rather than angry with them. Conversely, you also need to ensure that your child understands consequences of actions during this period of childhood, as this concept is much harder to acquire later in life.

Some families obtain a diagnosis for their child prior to starting school, but the majority of diagnoses occur after a child has already started school,[1] when teachers or other school staff may bring up the idea of having an autism spectrum diagnostic assessment for your child. As your child grows, knowing that they are not the only person who thinks, feels and interacts with the world in the way that they do can be very beneficial for their long-term mental well-being. Even if they do not have a diagnosis, they can feel very alone, even isolated and quite different.

If you live in a very small community, there may not be anyone there who is open about being on the autism spectrum. In this case, you may need to be more explicit about the differences that exist between children on all levels and not just communication or social differences. To be resilient, your child needs to know that they are valued and valuable human beings. It is very difficult to develop resilience if you only ever receive negative messages about yourself, whether those messages are verbalised or demonstrated in the way people interact with a child.

GETTING AND UNDERSTANDING A DIAGNOSIS IN CHILDHOOD

People usually pursue an autism spectrum diagnosis for their child because they would like support services in school or to access services from paraprofessionals like speech and language therapists or occupational

---

1   NCHS Data Brief 2012. Available at www.webmd.com/brain/autism/news/20120523/most-children-with-autism-diagnosed-at-5-or-older#1 (accessed 13 January 2017).

therapists. However, a diagnosis in itself can be useful, or it can put barriers in the way of an autistic child developing their potential. If you approach the process with the mindset that there is something wrong with your child, an autistic child, whether or not they use speech, is likely to pick up on that mindset. Instead, if you are focused on trying to understand your child to help them achieve their potential, this more positive attitude will be picked up on by the child and hopefully reflected by any professionals that you consult.

Depending on the age of your child, you may explain the whole process and the rationale behind the diagnosis or you may just explain that you are going to see someone to find out how to help your child enjoy life more and achieve their potential. Diagnosis cannot be seen to be a label of deficits or faults if it is going to be a positive and helpful part of your child's life journey. Instead, it can be talked about in terms of describing another aspect of your child, just like hair colour, eye colour, height, the language they understand and so on. When looking for professionals to carry out a diagnostic assessment of your child, try to use people who have this mindset and are not purely focused on deficits as there are a number of positive attributes to autism and being autistic.

You can explain the autism spectrum to your child in a number of different, age-appropriate ways, which focus on autism being a word that applies to people who think and experience the world in ways that are different to other people. You should explain that autistics – just like everyone else – have strengths and support needs. There are a number of children's books about autism now, as well as podcasts and videos featuring autistics and explaining different aspects of autism. You may find it useful to watch these first, as some of them are not supportive or helpful.

ACTIVITIES TO EXPLORE DIFFERENCE AND AUTISM POSITIVELY

Activity 1 – Diagnosis helps people understand your child's strengths and support needs

Draw all your family members, making sure to forget the glasses on the person who wears them. Ask your child what you forgot to draw for that person. Whether or not they respond with glasses, talk about how that person is short- or long-sighted and how, without their glasses, they struggle to do things that they can do more easily with their glasses on. Talk about other labels and descriptions for people, such as tall or short, and how each of these has individual strengths and difficulties in life.

Examples of strengths and support needs around height are being able to reach things easily whilst not being able to fit/reach other spaces. (If no-one in your family wears glasses, choose another attribute such as using a hearing aid or a wheelchair.)

Activity 2 – Explaining autism to your child in a positive and proactive manner

Use the word 'autism' with a neutral tone of voice, in the same way you would say 'orange' or 'cup'. Some autistic children do not hear tone of voice, whilst others are extremely sensitive to the tone of voice used. Other siblings and family members will interpret the way you talk about autism as the way in which they should talk about it and the way in which they should interact with autistic children.

Have the word 'autism' on a card, give it to your child and tell them what the word says (or, if they can read fluently, ask them to read it). Have some photos of people they may know, whether these are characters or real people, that portray autistics in a positive light as well as a photo of them and any other family members who are autistic. Tell your child that all these people share this word as a word that describes something about them, but that they all have other words, too. If your child is verbal, then name some of those other words, such as 'girl', 'short hair', 'glasses', 'uses a wheelchair', and so on.

Tell your child about how using the word 'autism' should help people to understand them better. (Do not say 'will' as even though it should, it doesn't always.) Introduce a couple of the things that they are good at and something related to their autism that they struggle with. Explain that autism is one of their characteristics that has resulted in those strengths and those support needs/difficulties. Be sure to let them know that they *can* and *will* learn things throughout their life. A really good video to watch on this is by Katy Kenah and can be found at the permalink: https://drive. google.com/file/d/0B46k8TylQ7MZVF85bmdvNVQ0SFU/view or at https://healthypossibilities.net/resources.

This video illustrates how changing language used around autism can powerfully highlight the possibilities for individuals rather than focusing on the struggles or challenges.

Activity 3 – Family time, me time and together time

It is important that autistic children, like any other children, do not 'rule the roost' and have resilience in the aspect of being able to accept other people's choices from time to time. It is not fair on any siblings or other family members for everyone to have to watch the same show on repeat for three years (although it is quite alright for an individual to do so if they so choose, without imposing that on everyone else).

Make a photo board with your child that has everyone in the family on it. Have a separate chart with the headings 'Family Time', 'Me Time' (or 'Alone Time') and 'Together Time'. Within this chart, you can place photos of family members and activities. For example, you might have a photo of eating breakfast and this has a photo of the whole family, so it would go in the family time section. A photo of Mum and a picture of the bath may go in the me/alone time section and so on. In this way, your child can see that each child has together time, family time and alone time, and siblings can feel confident that they can also have some special together time with a parent. This can prevent resentment building up in siblings who perceive that they never have special time with adult family members. This activity can also ensure that the adults in the home also have their own me time and together time, which can build resilience and foster positive relationships when things are difficult.

Activity 4 – Talking to your child's school/teachers about their diagnosis (or why you are taking your child for an autism spectrum assessment)

Sharing information about your child can really help schools to educate and support your child as effectively as possible. Although in years gone by there was a stigma associated with an autism spectrum diagnosis, this is rarely the case now. Teachers may even be able to add relevant information to the diagnostic assessment information, so that the assessment is as accurate as possible over multiple contexts.

If you choose to talk to the school/teacher, you can set the scene for the diagnosis as a positive and helpful thing. You can ensure that the diagnosis or assessment is viewed as enabling everyone to accurately use your child's strengths and interests to maximise their learning. You may want to take the diagnostic report with you to discuss or to have a plain language summary instead. In your discussions, it is good to talk about both areas of need and areas of strength, and to stress the personality and characteristics of your child as a well-loved and highly valued family member. Also, ask if the teacher would like any more information and then you can share any resources that you have found particularly helpful. Do not assume that the teacher is highly experienced or knowledgeable about autism, or conversely that they know nothing. Knowledge and skills around autism vary wildly from teacher to teacher:

> My son was not doing well as school; he was acting out a lot and quite angry. We had a meeting with the school, where I wanted to change the way they saw him. I talked about all the things he is good at and his teacher started to talk about his sense of humour and how funny he is. After this, we decided to review his sensory issues and work out what could be changed to help him stay calmer and what to do after he had a meltdown. It took some time, but he is doing much better now and the teachers are more understanding now they know about his autism diagnosis. Before that, I think they thought he was a wild child and I was a useless single dad. (John)

Activity 5 – Building your own resilience – meeting other autism parents and autistic adults

Parenting anyone is a hard job, no matter what their age or stage in life. It can be lonely or difficult when a parent feels isolated because of a perception that their child is different or not typical. This is one of the reasons why meeting other autism parents can be useful. However, one of the major stressors for parents is the worry about their child's future. This is where meeting a range of autistic adults can help build your resilience and enable you to see and hear the range of futures open to your child. It is important to remember that the verbal abilities of an autistic 5-year-old tell you nothing about their potential. Temple Grandin did not talk until she was 3½ years old.[2]

Activity 6 – Deciding who to tell what to – parents of children in your child's class

Some families report that after a few years in school, their child is the only one in the class who hasn't yet been to a classmate's birthday party, whilst other families say that their autistic child is well-accepted and included by their peers and the local community. Only you can judge how others will react to you and your child. However, being open about the positive ways to include your child may be a good start, as sometimes invites are not extended because the host doesn't think your child wants to be invited (because of media stereotypes of autistics as loners who don't want friends).

You can write a list of:

• Who do I want to talk to about my child's difficulties and strengths?

WHY?

• What will I tell them?

WHY?

Your child's teacher may have some useful ideas around this activity, too. Please note that your child has a right to privacy and you should not share things that will embarrass or humiliate them, for example do not post a video online of your child having a meltdown. In discussing your child with others, it is more useful and helpful to say things like: 'My son is autistic, he loves to play with Thomas the Tank Engine and is still learning to share, so if he comes to play I will bring two, one for him and one for your son.' Or: 'My daughter is on the autism spectrum, which means she can appear to be quite bossy because she likes to know what is happening. If she knows what is happening and is about to happen, she can often join in or watch quite happily whilst she becomes familiar with what people are doing.'

---

2   Grandin, T. (1996) *Emergence: Labelled Autistic*, reissue edition. New York: Warner Books.

BUILDING SELF-CONFIDENCE AND SELF-ESTEEM FOR AUTISTIC CHILDREN IS A CORE BUILDING BLOCK FOR RESILIENCE

For autistic children, self-confidence – that belief that you can do and can learn – is vital to the development of resilience and extremely useful in their journey through life. Without it, autistic children start to believe the stories they hear, that autistics cannot do anything or live fulfilling lives, or if they are doing something, some people will tell them that they are not 'really autistic'. A lack of self-confidence can be quite disabling, and families can ensure that the language they use builds confidence, by, for example, saying that their child 'does not yet' have a particular skill or knowledge set, rather than saying that they cannot do something. The use of 'yet' implies to both your child and others that your child is still able to learn to do whatever it is:

> When I had been at school about a year, the rest of my class were able to get changed before and after PE (gym class) all by themselves. However, I could not take my shoes off or put them back and do up the laces by myself. My teacher was so kind, she would often comment about how I had managed to take my socks off this time, or put my t-shirt on (even if it was back to front). She would always talk about how I just needed some more time and teaching to learn how to do it. I also heard her talk to Mum after school one day about how it might be easier for me to manage shoes that had Velcro or were slip-ons or had some kind of 'magic laces' that didn't need to be tied or untied. It made me feel so much more confident about trying each time to do part of the getting changed. (John)

As you can see from John's story, even 6-year-olds are aware of their developmental differences, but when they are responded to positively, they do not have any negative impact on the child. However, when these differences are highlighted negatively, autistic children can carry that with them for many years, even into adulthood:

> I was looking forward to learning to write at school, and, during my first year, I enjoyed all our writing activities, even though I found them really hard because it hurt holding the pencil. When I got into

the second year, my teacher got really angry with me. He said I was attention-seeking, whinging and trying to avoid work and that writing didn't really hurt my hand. This made me so anxious because I found it hard to do more writing as it hurt more and because I was anxious, my writing was not getting better and he wouldn't put my work up on the wall because he said it wasn't good enough, but everyone else's was up there, even if it wasn't perfect.

Ever since that, I have hated writing tasks, which seem to become all that school is about by the time you are about 9 or 10. Even as an adult I don't like to write, not because it hurts my hand, which it does, but because I don't want to do something that isn't good enough. (Alex)

Children do not need to be good at everything to have self-confidence, they just need to understand their strengths and how to use these to maximise their learning. These strengths do not have to be academic and may, at first glance, seem quite obscure. I am sure that many adults along the way thought that Temple Grandin's animal skills were not very useful. However, she became an important feedlot designer and makes a very good living engaged in doing work that she thoroughly enjoys and is very good at.

If your child does not speak yet, this does not mean that they have no skills, they may be very academic or not. Strengths are found by looking for what your child enjoys and/or does well. The following activity will help you to figure out and celebrate your child's strengths.

ACTIVITIES TO BUILD YOUR CHILD'S SELF-CONFIDENCE

Activity 1 – Building self-confidence – strengths

Every six months or so, from when your child first starts school (this can be done just before), really observe your child over a weekend to see what they do, how they spend their undirected time (what they choose to do) and how they respond to requests and instructions from you or other adults or other children. Make notes about these points and then rewrite them in a positive format. Then sit down with your child and share these strengths with them. Give them some examples of how they can use their strengths at home, in the classroom and in the playground. As they get older, ask them if they have any other strengths that you missed out, and how they can use these strengths. You can use a journal-type book to do this in so that you can keep a record of all their strengths throughout school. This can be a great source of positive input to build self-confidence.

Example format:

Date: How old………….. is……….

Strengths in free time/choice:

Communication strengths:

Strengths in interactions with others:

Strengths in learning:

How these strengths can be used:

At home –

In the classroom –

In the playground –

Activity 2 – Building self-confidence – being set up for success

Every child of every ability has something that they do well, whether it is drinking unaided or getting help for others when they hurt themselves or any other thing that you can think of. However, autistic children do not always want to try and learn new things as they often fear failure. Because of this, it is important to set them up for success for many of the things that they learn initially. This means that you can't just tell a child to clean their teeth, for example, you need to teach them how to do it. There are two techniques that are particularly useful for teaching in ways that set children up for success – backward chaining and forward chaining. Both of these involve detailed task analysis by the adult who is going to do the teaching/ chaining. The example given is for making a sandwich, which is a very useful skill for primary school autistic children, as they are more likely to eat something which they have made. In this example, we are going to use jam – if your child hates this, substitute it for something that they do eat. This can be done with gluten-free bread as well as regular bread:

- *Step 1* – Task analysis: In this example, what steps are involved in making a jam sandwich?

    1. Taking the bread bag out of the fridge (open fridge, take out, close fridge).

    2. Opening the bread bag.

    3. Taking out two slices of bread and putting them on a plate or bread board.

    4. Closing up the bread bag.

    5. Putting the bread back into the fridge (open fridge, put in, close fridge).

    6. Taking the jam jar out of the fridge (open fridge, take out, close fridge).

    7. Opening the jam jar.

    8. Taking a knife out of the cutlery drawer (open drawer, take out, close drawer).

    9. Putting a knife into the jam jar.

    10. Getting jam onto the knife.

    11. Taking the knife out of the jam jar whilst keeping jam on the knife blade.

    12. Spreading jam on *one* of the pieces of bread on *one* side.

    13. Putting the dirty knife in the kitchen sink or dishwasher (open dishwasher, put knife in, close dishwasher).

    14. Picking up the piece of bread without jam and putting it on top of the piece with jam so that the jam is on the inside of the two pieces.

- *Step 2* – Once you have done the task analysis, you can forward chain or backwards chain a task that you and your child are focused on, so that you do the initial steps or last steps and your child does the last or first step. As they are successful increase the number of steps that they do. Remember to ensure that they get to see the steps modelled before attempting them themselves. You can use verbal or picture prompts for each step in the task.

- *Step 3* – Praise and suggest whichever other part they do next time. Your child may want to do the first and last step, which is fine – you can do the middle steps.

- *Step 4* – Repeat until they can do the whole task. In this step, do not pressure them to complete it independently before they are ready but, equally, do not keep doing things for your child that they are capable of doing by themselves. If children require support to do one or two small steps and are otherwise able to manage, keep doing those steps for them and move on to step 5. Some children may have motor control or hand–eye co-ordination difficulties – which take time to develop and manifest themselves – and this should not be seen as a deficit. Instead, you should support the steps that your child requires support with and encourage independence in areas where this is feasible.

- *Step 5* – Do this again with another activity from steps 1–4 (this sequence can be used for any activity).

Activity 3 – Building self-confidence – being set up for independence and resilience

If your child can read, you can use written bullet points/a list for this activity. If not, then use photo prompts (if they cannot relate to photo prompts, you may need models of each step or use a video that they can pause and restart at each step).

Get your child to do an activity that you *know* they can successfully do from Activity 2 above with their written/picture/video prompts. Try *not* to give them extra prompts unless they seem to be getting anxious or distressed, in which case praise them for the steps that they have completed so far and direct them to where they are on their prompt sheet/ video. It can be helpful to have written/picture prompt sheets laminated so that your child can cross out or tick each step as they complete it. This is particularly useful where children are still developing sequencing skills and/or executive functioning. If they complete the task and do not have the expected outcome, help them to go through the steps and see what they missed out. Do *not* catastrophise or put all your focus on the error. Instead, simply comment that the situation can probably be fixed if you both work out the missing step and redo it from there:

> I never really understood that you could fix something up if it went wrong. I just thought things were either right or they were wrong, in which case they were wrong forever. I was about 8 when I went swimming with school and I lost my knickers in the changing room. I was absolutely devastated and cried and screamed and yelled. I don't think the teacher had any idea why I was so upset, and she was trying to get us all to hurry up to get on the bus to go back to school. This girl next to me said, 'Why don't you just put your swimsuit back on but leave the top rolled down under your skirt?' I was just amazed that anyone could find a solution to things going wrong. Once I stopped crying, she told me that she always put her clothes in her backpack so that she couldn't lose things because she had lost her knickers once when she went swimming with her mum. I hadn't ever thought about putting my clothes in my backpack as I was taking them off, I had always just dropped them on the floor. (Lara)

If Lara had been talked to differently, she may not have learnt these valuable lessons in resilience, which are that you can learn from mistakes and that mistakes are not usually the end of the world. However, even the smallest negative throwaway comment can impede the development of self-confidence in autistic children and damage their sense of self. When autistic children hear that they cannot do something or that they will never be able to do something, they often take it to heart and, because they believe it to be true, they will never try. There are a few autistic children who have high levels of resilience and self-confidence who are unaffected by negative comments from others, or use them as motivators to achieve that exact thing, but this is rare and is not a recommended strategy:

I only used to eat crackers and chocolate milk, and I needed other people to open these for me. This was fine for the first few years, but then the other kids in my class started to tease me about not being able to open my own lunch, or they would spill all the milk when they opened it. If I asked the teacher, they usually said they were too busy and I should ask someone else. I don't know why people were so mean to me about such a small thing. It made me really sad, and I often didn't eat anything at all at school, and then Mum got cross with me that I was bringing my lunch home uneaten. So, in Year 4 at school, I started throwing my lunch in the bin instead of eating it. I still need help at age 20 to open cartons or packets, but my support workers are really good about asking me if I want to try or if I want them to open it for me. (Josh)

AUTISTIC ROLE MODELS FOR CHILDREN AND PARENTS

The value of having autistic role models for autistic children is that these people understand how an autistic child thinks, experiences the world and autistic ways of responding to the world. Having autistic adults involved in the lives of autistic children is important to role model living successfully as an autistic. These adults can help non-autistic parents to understand the all-encompassing nature of autism and how much autistics change and develop over the years, just like all other people!

WHO CAN BE ROLE MODELS?

Autistic role models can be relatives or friends of the family who are autistic adults, or even autistic children who are a few years older than your child. They can also be public figures or celebrities who are autistic, like the singer Susan Boyle or the actor Dan Ackroyd. Even if your child is not aware of these people's work, you can explain to them that this person is a successful actor (or musician or physicist, etc.) and that they are autistic, too.

There is a saying: 'If you can't see it, you can't be it,' meaning that not being aware of any autistic people who have a job or an education or are parents or any number of other socially valued roles can mean that autistic children have no concept of their own capability. Autistic role models play a vital role in setting a positive example of what is possible for autistic children, and having them in your child's life helps to build their understanding of what they can achieve, and also helps normalise autistic experience and focus on the great potential that autistic people have.

Both of the authors of this book have had too many experiences of autistic children and teenagers being stunned that we work, and expressing the misconception that autistic adults cannot work. This is simply not true. For some autistic adults, work may require a large amount of support and for others a minimal amount of support. It is impossible to say what the case is for your child as the developmental trajectory of autistics does not follow any typical pattern. For example, Temple Grandin, a world-famous professor, did not talk until many years after typically developing children begin talking.

CREATING AN AUTISTIC PEER GROUP FOR YOUR CHILD

Autistic children benefit from an autistic peer group because they are more likely to feel comfortable and at ease around other autistic children. However, it is important to note that just because children are autistic, it does not automatically mean that they will get on, just as two Japanese people living in France may or may not get on!

Many years ago, when I was teaching a multi-age class, I had two groups that I was responsible for, and within the two groups of students, there were two autistic children. I was meant to merge the two groups into one in the afternoon, but in all good conscience I couldn't. Those two children couldn't stand each other. If they had to be in the same room, they would both scream non-stop until they were separated again. Both students were lovely, with their own different strengths and challenges, but put them together and it was just intolerable for everyone. I found it interesting that previous teachers did not have an issue with this and regularly combined the two groups and then complained about the screaming. Over time, the two became able to tolerate each other but they never got on. (Emma)

I was not diagnosed as being on the autism spectrum until I was 20, but I met a number of kids in both primary and secondary school whom I think were almost certainly autistic. One of these children was one of my best friends at primary school, Paul. Paul was quirky and clever. He put pepper on everything, including cake. Paul's passion was castles. He made detailed scale models of castles which were quite beautiful. Paul often copped some teasing and bullying, as did I. We became each other's ally. I remember people saying Paul was my boyfriend but he wasn't. We were each other's mutual support. Our friendship sometimes protected us from being victimised and, when it didn't, we had each other to talk to about it. Paul and I 'got' each other. I had no other friendships like that until recently. (Jeanette)

An autistic peer group can include any autistic children who your child is comfortable around. They may be a little younger or older and do not need to be the exact same age as your child. In actuality, many autistic children prefer people who are a number of years younger or older. This group may be run by an organisation or be an informal group that gets together from time to time. Both have their places and uses and it will depend on where you live and your access to other families with autistic children and autism organisations.

Autism, if you are not autistic, is most easily understood as a different culture. Autistics of all ages have particular (individual) ways of experiencing the world, understanding the world and making sense of things. These differ from non-autistics or allistics,[3] and are neither better nor worse, they just are. In the same way that the Dutch have a culture that encapsulates the way people interact with each other and what is valued and promoted, and this is different from the Japanese way of interacting and so on, so it is with autistics. Autistics overwhelmingly seem to have a huge sense of social justice based on the idea of equality of all (people and/or people and animals and things). They tend to struggle to filter sensory input and tend not to prioritise human voices and faces as allistics do, which creates a number of behavioural differences, including communication differences. Within this overall autistic culture, each individual varies, just as people within other cultures are not all exactly the same.

---

3   Non-autistic people.

DIFFERENCES BETWEEN HOME AND SCHOOL

It is important to understand that your child's school persona and home persona can differ. For autistic children (and adults), context can influence mood, confidence and so on, resulting in completely different behaviour at home and at school. For some children, this can result in them having lots of meltdowns/challenges in one setting and none in the other. It is not always the case that school is where the difficulties are. Some children manage all day in class and then, as soon as they get picked up or arrive at home, seem to go to pieces.

One of the ways to understand why this happens is to look at a day in the life of your autistic child through the lens of spoon theory. Spoon theory was developed by Christine Miserandino to help explain what it is like to live with lupus. In spoon theory, everyone starts out with the same number of spoons, which are refreshed every night. People lose a spoon when they have to do something physically or mentally exhausting. In the autistic version of spoon theory, autistics also lose spoons when they are deluged by sensory input and/or emotional input, including anxiety.[4]

If you are using spoon theory to understand your child, allocate them ten hypothetical spoons, represented by your fingers. Hold your fingers and thumbs up in the air. Now, picture an average morning, right from when your child wakes up or is woken up. For every physical, mental, sensory or emotional challenge encountered by your child throughout the day, they lose a spoon, so you put down a finger/thumb. A meltdown/ shutdown is guaranteed if they have no spoons left. They may gain a spoon if they are able to engage in a preferred activity around their passion, or favoured sensory experience for a significant amount of time. Otherwise, they cannot gain spoons.

SPOON THEORY EXAMPLE

The alarm goes off and Jake gets up, determined to make his mum happy by being ready for school on time. As he gets out of bed, he stands on some Lego *(lose a spoon)*, which really hurts. Jake only screamed for a short time on the way to the bathroom to have his

---

4   Information on spoon theory. Available at: https://cdn.totalcomputersusa. com/butyoudontlooksick.com/uploads/2010/02/BYDLS-TheSpoonTheory. pdf

morning shower and go to the toilet, clean his teeth and brush his hair. Only, when Jake got to the bathroom, the door was shut and it wouldn't open even when he turned the handle and pushed really hard. Instead, his big sister Lisa shouted at him to wait, she'd only be a few more minutes *(lose a spoon)*. Jake waited and waited, thinking about how many minutes were in a few, two or three or four or more. It became clear that Lisa either could not count, or a few was more than five. Jake started to panic that he would not have time to do everything *(lose a spoon)*. Finally, Lisa came out, and she pushed him to get past *(lose a spoon)*. Jake went into the bathroom and slipped on the wet floor *(lose a spoon)*. He tried to have a shower, but the water was not warm enough *(lose a spoon)*. Jake was so frustrated, he would be late and not clean, and it wasn't his fault. He heard Mum yelling at him to hurry up or he wouldn't have time for breakfast *(lose a spoon)*. Jake put his clothes on and rushed into the kitchen. Mum took one look at him and started yelling about showers and hair or something. Jake started screaming *(lose a spoon)*. Mum stopped yelling and asked Jake to sit down and eat his toast and marmalade. But when Jake sat down, he saw Lisa had had a bite of his toast *(lose a spoon)*.

In this example story, Jake has not even left the house for school yet and has already used up nine of his ten spoons!

During workshops when this activity of viewing autistic children through spoon theory is used, many parents and teachers are surprised by how many children have no spoons left by the time they arrive at school. This can be one reason why young children find the transition to school difficult in the mornings – they are all out of spoons.

If you are finding this hard to understand, remember, your young child has not yet learnt all the strategies to manage their environment that they will master over the coming years. When a toddler runs away to hide under the blankets, they may well be demonstrating an excellent coping strategy. However, many parents struggle to let their children use these sorts of coping mechanisms whilst still ensuring that the children arrive at school on time!

COMMUNICATING ISSUES AT HOME TO THE SCHOOL

If your child has had some difficulties at home and is going to be arriving at school with unresolved issues or worries, then it is very helpful for the school to know this. However, it is not always appropriate or helpful to be passing information to staff members when you are trying to drop your child off at school. One of the most helpful strategies is to work out what type and frequency of communication your child's teacher would find most effective.

Some teachers are happy to text and receive texts, though many are not, especially where this involves giving out their personal mobile phone numbers. Likewise, some teachers check emails two or three times a day and find this effective, whereas others find it very impersonal and fraught with potential misunderstandings. If you are trying to check in personally with the teacher every day, you need to understand that this may have an impact on the way that they like to greet or say goodbye to the students, and that there may be up to 29 other sets of parents wanting to talk with the teacher, too. Instead, it might be better for you to ask the teacher how they would like to be informed about any important issues in the mornings and how they would like to let you know anything important that has happened during the day.

If there are some major difficulties at home or impending changes, it can be useful to request a meeting with the school to discuss how these difficulties or changes may affect your child and what strategies you could all use during that time. For example, if your child has shared custody arrangements, it can help the school and your child to know exactly when and where the child will be going to/coming from each day. Some children can become very distressed if they forget who will be picking them up at the end of the school day, in which case having a photo of the person who will pick them up on their desk or in their pocket during the day can be very helpful.

If your child suffers from constipation, it is important to share the signs of this with the school so that they can anticipate a lower frustration threshold, for example, which often occurs with constipation. Be very factual in your approach and your information sharing, and remember that prefacing information with a small greeting or genuine enquiry about how they are doing will help the teacher to feel valued by you.

Some changes in life that may (or may not!) cause large behavioural changes are:

- moving house

- a new sibling being born

- parent's movements changing (parent starts a new job or different working hours)

- starting school

- a friend moving away or going to a different school.

During school hours, the school has responsibility for the children at that school. How this is phrased varies from country to country, but in effect the teachers are substitute parents during school hours. Because of this, the responsibility for understanding and addressing any issues that arise for each child lies with the school. However, it is rarely possible for this to be effective without strong collaboration between the school and the family. Each school district/area will have their own policies about how this collaboration should look, but this does not mean that you are restricted to just that.

As your child grows, they should be involved in planning meetings with teachers and family that are about their needs. Your child should be encouraged to share their views and opinions on their school experiences and help set learning goals. Even quite young children can be involved in this process and there are several ways in which children who do not use speech and can't yet write or draw well can be involved. For example, using a smartphone, tablet or camera, a child can take photos of things they love and things they find difficult or want help with.

When encouraging your child to identify and articulate their feelings about any school issues, it is very important to talk about how other people's feelings can be hurt by the way in which things are said. Talk about the difference between identifying problems and blaming someone. Resilience is best fostered by a solution-seeking mindset, as it is irrelevant who causes a problem once the problem is solved, but seeking to lay blame can raise barriers to collaboration.

ACTIVITIES TO BUILD SCHOOL RESILIENCE

Activity 1 – Sorting out communication with your child's school

This activity is more for you than your child, but fostering a respectful and collaborative relationship with your child's teachers will make school a more pleasant or positive experience for everyone. Ask for a meeting, set parameters of time if this has never been done before and take the following questions with you.

An example of setting out parameters with your child's school is: Would you prefer us to contact you:

- In person?

- By text?

- By email?

- Other?

In the mornings at drop-off/pick-up, is it okay to pass a note or have a quick catch-up or would you prefer that we make an appointment to talk in person?

As a family, we can reply to texts usually within ...., emails within ...., and for us .... is the best day/time to have face-to-face meetings. We like to make sure that our child only hears supportive conversations about him, so please do not tell us when things have gone wrong face to face if .... is in the vicinity. We would prefer a text, email or note to be given to us if things have been difficult in the day. Many thanks, The .... family.

Activity 2 – Strengths and support needs

Help your child to identify and record orally, visually or in some other way:

- one thing they enjoy at school

- one thing they are good at, at school

- and one thing they would like more help with at school.

Model this with things in your own life, either from work or the home. Once you have modelled (using words or drawings or photos), involve your child in identifying something at home in each of these areas. For many autistics, they enjoy what they are good at, but this is not always the case. Do not criticise or ask for a second thing as this will send a message that you do not value your child's own reflections.

Ask your child to share these opinions with her teacher. It is okay to practise this at home first if it will help you and her to feel more comfortable.

WHAT DOES RESILIENCE LOOK LIKE AT THIS LIFE STAGE?

- A resilient child will be able to ask for help from parents, teachers or other trusted, responsible adults, whether or not they use speech.

- They will have a growing ability to manage change.

- They will be able to say 'no' or challenge requests or commands to do something that the child knows to be wrong. This is more complex than it sounds as autistic children can think that things are wrong that other people perceive as just fine! You should never ask your autistic child *if* they want to do something unless you are willing to accept and respect their answer of 'no'.

- Your child sees themselves in a largely – or increasingly – positive light.

- Your child is willing to take on new challenges or activities, even if they need some support to do so.

- Your child initiates new activities or games with familiar people.

WHAT IMPEDES RESILIENCE AT THIS LIFE STAGE?

Even young children can face barriers to developing resilience. The biggest of these for autistic children can be anxiety. Anxiety is very real, but children need supporting to learn how to manage their anxiety so that it does not limit their life. Anxiety is often present when autistic children do not know what is happening or going to happen next. Using visuals to show what is happening now and next can be very useful to help manage and minimise anxiety for autistic children. Some autistic children do not respond well to visuals and some prefer just to be explicitly and accurately told what is happening and going to happen next.

If autistic children get accurate and reliable information from their parent(s), they develop confidence in the trustworthiness of their parent(s). If, on the other hand, they lose or never develop this trust, it can make the world a more overwhelming place and seriously impede their ability to build resilience. Accurate and reliable means always saying what you mean and meaning what you say. For example, if you say that dinner is in 5 minutes, it *must* be in 5 minutes. It can be easier to say that dinner is almost ready and will be ready in between 1 and 10 minutes. Again, if you have set bedtimes in your family, these should be set and not changed all the time.

This anxiety can be at the heart of fear of change, which is more a fear of the unknown, unless you have always been very routine-oriented, which can create routine dependency:

> I was convinced for much of my life that most adults couldn't tell the time. Teachers would say it was playtime in 5 minutes, and then 5 minutes later they would say it was in a few more minutes, and they could never explain how many a few was. I still get anxious and frustrated about time as people just don't use it properly. My mum could tell the time – my bedtime was 7.00 p.m. with lights out at 7.30 p.m., and she did this every night until I was 14, when it moved to 8.00 p.m. I liked knowing that I could read in bed for half an hour each night, it was lovely. (Luke)

Self-doubt is one of the banes of an autistic existence! This can have its roots in early childhood or be acquired later in life. Self-doubt can crowd out resilience if it becomes the dominant thought pattern of the autistic child. Because of the perseverative thinking style of autistics (where they think about and analyse things over and over), it is important to teach young autistics that it is really not the end of the world when things go wrong. Ensure that your autistic child knows that mistakes and difficulties are learning experiences, which, though challenging at the time, are worth it afterwards. Jeanette Purkis's autobiography *Finding a Different*

Kind of Normal demonstrates this in an adult context. The author made a large number of significant errors and poor choices, many of which had consequences for her and for people she knew and loved. However, she used these negative experiences to drive positive changes in her character and life.

Bullying or other invalidating experiences can occur in the home or by extended family, or at school or other places. The more of these that are experienced, the more difficult it can be for a child to develop resilience. Bullying and discrimination are forms of invalidating experiences, as are having too low expectations, which are based on the belief that the child is less able than they are. This is a particular problem for autistic children who do not (yet) speak as they are often assumed to be far less capable than they really are. Too high expectations can be invalidating for young children too, who can begin to feel like failures if they can never reach the targets set for them. This is most common where autistic children are average or above average in some skills and struggle in other areas.

WHAT ARE PROTECTIVE FACTORS FOR RESILIENCE AND HOW DO YOU INSTIL THEM IN YOUR CHILD?

Much as there are risk factors that make it harder for a child to acquire resilience, there are also some very effective protective factors. Where these things are present, your child is more likely to build and maintain resilience.

Protective factors for resilience among autistic children (and adults) include the following.

Self-acceptance

Accepting oneself and building their confidence can assist your child's ability to take on new challenges. Self-acceptance is an attitude that can be modelled by parents and other adult carers. This can be a combination of demonstrating support for and valuing your child and behaving in a way that demonstrates that you value yourself as well. Self-acceptance should be based on a clear awareness and understanding of one's own strengths and areas of struggle or difficulty in a non-judgemental manner. It is important not to confuse self-acceptance with the need to be perfect, which is an impossibility for anyone.

An assumption of competence

One issue that autistic people experience – and those with other health conditions or disability, too – is an assumption by significant people in their life that they are incompetent or incapable of achieving what others do. This assumption is often driven by broader attitudes in society around autism. It starts from being something external to your child but they will most likely internalise it and believe themselves less capable than their typically developing peers if they hear and see this attitude being expressed around or about them.

Contrary to this assumption of incompetence, you can instil in your child an assumption of *competence*. Instead of focusing on what your child can't do, build their confidence and self-perception that they are competent and capable. If they want to try something new, support them to do that where possible. This does not mean ignoring their limitations but it does involve challenging the widely held view that all autistic children are unable to do what other children their age do.

Social/emotional support

Children who are – and feel – supported in family life and social settings with friends or family and relatives have a good base to build from in terms of their life skills, including resilience. Social and emotional support are great protective factors for resilience. While a lack of emotional support from family is a risk factor for invalidation, social and emotional support can be great validating factors helping children to build their resilience from a place of safety.

Positive reinforcement for good work or positive behaviour

Positive reinforcement is a great protective factor around acquiring resilience. It can effectively build positive self-image and confidence to try new things. Praise your child for doing good work or behaviour in different areas of their life (relationships with siblings, schoolwork, after school activities, etc.). This does not mean that you should ignore everything else, but that you should praise when deserved and note skills and concepts that your child needs to develop further. Over time, you will gain an understanding of when your child is being naughty versus when they are not sure what to do and chose something inappropriate, or they were in a state of sympathetic nervous system escalation and acted instinctively.

Caring/respectful friend(s)

Your school-age child may have some friends. Whom your child becomes friends with can be concerning for parents and often you do not have a lot of say in the matter. Friends who are caring and respectful of themselves and your child can be a great protective factor for resilience as they can model and share positive qualities with your child and provide support. As your child becomes older, you will need to help them understand in age-appropriate ways that not all people are good and kind and not all interactions are friendships.

Supportive, safe and understanding home environment

As discussed earlier in this book, a supportive and safe home environment where parents and siblings understand and respect the autistic child is a great start in life that will help build resilience and self-respect. This home environment can be the basis of the place of safety that will help support them through their life – and resilience – journey.

A level of responsibility

Resilience and responsibility are related. The act of taking on responsibility for a school aged autistic child can be a great way to scaffold resilience and social responsibility as they grow older. There are several ways in which a school age child can take on an appropriate level of responsibility, which include looking after pets, doing chores and helping with the care of younger siblings. Children should be involved in helping out in the home, or they can develop an expectation that others should always do everything for them:

> My dad used to have a farm when I was a child. We only got a small amount of pocket money, and when I wanted more money I would have to do some chores on the farm. None of the jobs was onerous – they usually involved making packing boxes for vegetables that were going to be sold.

I didn't particularly like working, but it wasn't too bad. When I got older and started work for real, I was told by my managers what an amazing work ethic I had. I thought about this and realised that the chores I did on the farm meant I understood the concept of needing to work when you need money. I have been a diligent employee ever since. (Ellie)

Child is stretched or challenged to do something new or more challenging

A protective factor for resilience is the idea of stretching somebody to take on something a little more challenging or a new activity. In fact, this concept of stretching is at the core of acquiring resilience. A resilient person takes on new challenges or more difficulty and learns from this. This, in turn, builds their ability to take on more challenges or not to be too concerned when new or more difficult challenges arise. The controlled challenges discussed in this book represent that stretching. Things may not always go to plan with stretching. Sometimes, the challenges will be too difficult or your child will have a setback. However, that does not mean that you – or your child – should give up. Stretching and challenging needs to be done in a supportive manner and if there is a setback, stop, debrief with your child and reassess the approach.

Positive self-identity as an autistic person

Many of the risk factors around resilience and autism stem from a lack of understanding of autism or prejudice against autistic people, focusing only on deficits. Autistic people can experience insecurity, self-doubt and self-hatred when they perceive autism negatively because of the things that they hear and the way that others treat them.

Helping your child to build their positive identity and self-perception as an autistic person is incredibly valuable. Not only does this have an impact on acquiring resilience, but it has positive flow-on effects to almost every element of your child's life. Helping your child to view themselves in a positive light and to see autism as an intrinsic part of their character, with strengths and support needs like any other person has, is very helpful. This is preferable to having a child despising themselves for being different. These positive thoughts and attitudes are a pretty great gift you can give your child.

CHAPTER 6

LIFE EVENTS FOR AUTISTIC CHILDREN AGES SEVEN TO TEN

Strategies and Activities around Building Resilience

This chapter will focus on a number of life events and developmental milestones that autistic children aged 7–10 years old are likely to experience, and that can help develop confidence and resilience. It will include a description of the life event and what specific issues it might pose for autistic children. Each milestone will also include information on what a good outcome might look like, as well as activities and strategies that parents can put in place to help their child develop resilience and set the foundations for independence through navigating through that life event.

CHANGES AT SCHOOL – OF TEACHER/ CLASS/CLASSROOM

By the time a child has reached 7 and older, whether they attend mainstream school, a specialist autism-specific or other specialist class or school or another place, it is likely that they have worked out some kind of understanding and routine of attending school. They will probably understand that they need to attend school and do coursework and homework. They will have some idea of the social setup in their class and school more broadly. They are likely to have picked up on some of the discipline and structure of the classroom. In short, the idea of going to school and what happens when they are there will most likely be familiar to them.

This familiarity often occurs due to explicit teaching that pre-school and junior primary/elementary school teachers use to teach young children the hidden curriculum. If autistic children don't get this explicit teaching, then they struggle to understand the social world of school even after a number of years.

However, by ages 7 and up, many autistic children may have some expectations around school. A child may have had the same teacher or been in the same classroom for some time. Routine can be supportive and soothing to many children, although *only* if the child can manage change. Children can still be impacted negatively by any unexpected changes to their daily routine or any planned changes that they are not prepared for.

As children go through school, changes to the classroom, class members, teachers or even school campuses can be difficult to manage. The very routine that you as a parent have worked hard with your child to make a part of your daily life and which has been a support and a protective factor against some of the other difficulties that can arise at school, can become a significant drawback to your child's resilience and confidence when it changes. Managing change is one of the key issues for autistic people – children and adults – and setting children up to be better able to cope with a change in routine is a very good step along their journey to resilience and independence.

It is important to convey the message that a change does not mean everything changes, that some change is positive and that anxiety around change can be disproportionate to the actual impact on your child's well-being when the change occurs. This is a difficult message to convey and it will need to be an ongoing discussion throughout childhood teen years and early adulthood, as many autistics worry that change is catastrophic.

For autistic people, routine can be a way of making sense of a frightening and confusing world. Autistic people understandably tend to latch onto routines and habits as these are predictable and can help them to feel safe in a world that comes across as frightening, confusing and hostile. Always keep this in mind when working through change with your autistic child. Your child is not being deliberately difficult in insisting on the same foods, clothes or television programmes. These things are an anchor point in a changing world. If those are taken away, they can panic about feeling safe as they have lost their predictability.

While you are at home, it is a lot easier to continue with routines. You can record every single episode of the TV programme your child loves and your child can watch them when they need to. You cannot, however, stop a teacher from taking on a new role or a school from merging two classes into one. But for your autistic child, the impact of the change at school may be huge. It is important to try and view changes in routine from your child's perspective and work with them to build strategies. Change is inevitable in life and you cannot shield your child from it, so it is a necessary lesson, but it is almost always going to be a difficult experience to teach.

If children do not learn to manage change when they are young, they can become routine dependent, which makes adult life very difficult, as life is not routine. For example, buses do not usually run on time, so if a young adult is routine dependent and their bus doesn't come on time, this can cause a meltdown. This would mean that this young adult is unemployable, unless they can learn to contain or manage their meltdowns. Remember – predictability is the key!

ACTIVITIES AROUND CHANGE AND UNDERSTANDING WHAT IS HAPPENING NEXT
Activity 1 – Talking about changes at school

By the time your child is 7 or older, they will have actually gone through some changes at school but they may no longer be focused on them. Talk to your child about their previous teachers and classmates, and how things changed and it was okay in the end. Go through artwork and writing they did when they're younger and talk about how they went through a change to be able to produce the work they can now. Talk about the different teachers they have had and explain that in the future, like they did in the past, these things about school will change again and it will be okay. This often works best before the change occurs rather than after a large change. If your child has already been through the change and struggled a lot, then it will be harder to instil the message that change can be okay.

Activity 2 – Open questions

If you know a change is coming up (new teacher, change of year level, etc.), talk to your child about their expectations and any concerns. Your child can ask any question about the new situation and what they think it will be like. Ask your child one question about their concerns and then give them the chance to ask a question about the change or related topics. No question is 'wrong'. This will not only help your child understand the change at school better but it also gives you a chance to understand what their concerns are and work with them to manage the change. It also helps give your child a sense of agency, which is very useful in building resilience.

Activity 3 – Road map

Work with your child to create a pictorial or written representation of how they see the change before it happens. What will the new classroom look like? How many kids will there be? What is the teacher's name? Through doing this activity together, try to ascertain your child's points of concern. After the change has occurred, revisit your child's road map together and add what has changed and anything that is worrying or difficult.

Activity 4 – Change timelines and diary

As the change approaches, draw up a timeline. Add on it events you know will happen on whatever days where possible. Each day, with your child, talk about what happened – what was different? Was it positive or negative? What did your child do in response to it? Are they worried about it? What do they want to happen? Keep adding to the timeline for as long as there are issues with the transition. As you complete it with your child, you can reflect with them on anything they are learning. This approach can work for other changes, too.

Activity 5 – Video modelling successful changes/transitions

Video modelling is a sort of video version of a Social Story™ that you create with your child as the star and the use of some creative editing, so that the video only shows your child achieving what you are wanting them to achieve. With mobile phones and tablets, anyone can use video modelling at home or at school. Software such as iMovie is really simple to use, making the editing quite easy.

If you want your child to manage going to bed at night without stress and anxiety, you might make a video of them going into their bedroom and getting ready for bed, then having a bedtime story read to them and then them asleep. This may take several nights to achieve, and you would edit out all the parts where they were not transitioning successfully. You would then record audio over the top to describe what your child is doing well. For example, 'Tim is ready for bed. Tim puts his pyjamas on when he is tired. Mum reads Tim a bedtime story. Tim relaxes during story and then Tim goes to sleep. Tim likes going to bed so his body can rest and be ready for the next day.'

Your child could then watch the video as and when they want or just after dinner a couple of times a week for a few weeks.

You can make any number of videos about changes and transitions that your child is struggling with. As they see themselves achieving these things, they are set up for success and learn that others believe in them.

Some signs that your child is doing well with changes in school include:

- Decreasing anxiety levels, particularly around school.

- Behaviour at school is not noticeably very different after the change to the way it was before.

- When your child talks about school, talking about the change and unpacking it does not comprise the entire conversation.

- No more or decreasing school refusal or absences after the change.

SCHOOL EXPECTATIONS – ACQUIRING NEW SKILLS

Acquiring new skills through practice is a highly valuable life skill for everyone, including autistic children. Being able to put one's mind to an activity or skill and build on previous understanding is vital in many areas of life, including education, employment, friendships and relationships, and in practical life skills like managing money.

Many autistic people find it difficult to acquire new skills. This is not necessarily because they lack the capability to do so. Rather, the process of going from beginner to novice to expert is not understood or adequately explained. An autistic child may see an example of a piece of work the teacher shows the class, which was completed by the teacher, and think that is how their first attempt at this task should look. The idea of practice or ongoing learning can be alien to autistic children. This is not to say that they cannot acquire skills through practice, but that they do not have a concept in their mind that it might take several attempts at a task to become confident and skilled at that task.

This issue can be bound up in perfectionism and anxiety. It can also relate to a child's sense of identity. If they do have some 'twice exceptional', 'gifted' or 'savant' skills, their positive identity might centre around their ability to do certain tasks without instruction or practice. However, it is very unlikely that a child will be gifted in every area of school. This could lead to them avoiding activities they are not good at, which compounds difficulty in learning new skills. In some cases, the solution is simply to explain the practice that most people go through in order to achieve proficiency:

When I was about 7, my mum offered to teach me to knit. My mum is an excellent knitter and makes wonderful clothes and hats and even a nativity scene one year. I remember her sitting in her chair knitting. She could carry on a conversation while making complex patterns and the 'click, click' of her knitting needles was always an even rhythm and very comforting. Presumably, my mum has not always been such a great knitter. I understand now that she must have learnt to knit from somebody. But when I was a child, I knew my mum could knit and I couldn't. So, when she offered to teach me I was delighted. I assumed I would instantly be able to sit and knit jumpers and socks and things and they would be beautiful.

My mum gave me a pair of knitting needles and some yarn. She showed me what to do to make the stitches and then the next one. I was horrified at how difficult it was. My mum just sat there and garments emerged as if by magic from her quick hands, but for me, all I had was about five rows of black wool with holes from many dropped stitches. I felt betrayed and confused and that was the last time I picked up a pair of knitting needles! Even now, I am in my 40s, and I struggle to take on a task I find difficult. (Millie)

Some signs that your child is doing well with changes in school include:

- They stick at doing something that requires practice.

- They ask for your assistance with an activity they are practising.

- There are no/fewer meltdowns, shutdowns or refusals to attend an activity that requires practice (sports, music lessons, etc.)

- They become more enthusiastic about an activity they needed to practise.

- They communicate that they enjoy or want to do an activity they have been practising.

- You notice they are transferring skills and attitudes from one thing requiring practice to another.

ACTIVITIES TO ENHANCE SCHOOL RESILIENCE

Activity 1 – Talking about practice

Initiate a conversation with your child about things that they need to practice. Use examples from your own life. Talk about your child being a baby and then a toddler, a little kid and their age now. If possible, get them to reflect on how they have grown into their ability to do things through getting older and learning new skills. Reflect this back to new tasks or learning.

Activity 2 – Teaching the adult

Most autistic people – including children – have a passion or 'special interest'. Often, parents hear a lot about this interest from their child but they may not understand it in the way in which their child does. In this activity, ask your child to teach you about their passion or interest. You can set some parameters around time, as children – and adults – can be very keen to share knowledge of their passion with a willing audience. So, maybe give your child a time limit to the lesson. At the end, tell your child how much you have learned about their interest but that you still need to find out more to be an expert.

Have a few more 'lessons' with your child and then tell them what you have learned. Emphasise the fact that you did not know much at the start but are now proficient and the lessons from your child helped you to go from newbie to expert! Then reflect this back onto their experience of acquiring new skills.

SOCIAL INTERACTIONS IN SCHOOL

For autistic children, social interaction can be challenging. Other children can be seen as unpredictable, confusing, rude, invasive or inconsistent. As autistic children grow older, they often become aware of differences between themselves and typically developing children, and they may feel that they are doing social interactions 'all wrong'. Allegiances can shift and change for no apparent reason, and an autistic child may find themselves losing friendships and having no idea why. Autistic children can be quite blunt or literal, which can be misinterpreted as rudeness and they may find it hard to 'let things slide'. They may seem odd or shy to other children. Autistic children are often very keen for social interactions and friendships, but struggle when in the company of other children. They may prefer the company of children who are much younger or older than them or prefer the company of adults to that of children of their own age.

Autistic children often form friendships with other autistic children or children with other neurological differences such as ADHD or dyslexia. A shared sense of a 'different' identity and similarities in experience can happen in these situations. In addition, autistic people can be understood as a culture, with their own 'language' and customs. This could be why autistic children may bond with other autistic children. It should be noted, however, that all autistic children will not naturally be friends with all other autistic children. They are individuals as all children are.

There is a perception among some people that autistic children do not want or need social connectedness and friends, and/or that they are incapable of forging and keeping friendships. These beliefs are incorrect, although many autistic children – and adults – often want and need less social time than their non-autistic peers. Friendships are as important to foster for autistic children as they are for anyone else. Autistic children can be bullied, excluded and rejected socially, and this can lead to anxiety around social activities and forming friendships. Sometimes, children who are perceived as friends can be a negative influence on your child, encouraging them to engage in poor behaviour or using your child as the unknowing butt of jokes. It is important for an autistic child to have enough social contact and for that social contact to be positive and affirming, as positive interpersonal connectedness is the single biggest protective factor in terms of mental health.

It is a hard call for parents to know what is going on at school in terms of social interaction and also to determine which friends are a positive, helpful and supportive person in your child's life and those who are not. This is one area where it is very important for parents to have a dialogue with their child in whatever way works. If your child is willing and able, and comfortable discussing (using whatever communication they use) with you what is happening at school and what they are doing with their friends, this makes it considerably easier for you to know what sorts of social interactions they are having and whether they are helpful or damaging.

Some autistic children do not seem interested in friends or social connection. They will play by themselves in the school yard and not accept any offers of friendship. Some autistic children grow into social activity. So, if they do not want a friend at 7 years old, they might at 9. However, there is a difference between a child being happily not social and allowed to entertain themselves in the playground and a child who does not want friends but is being bullied. Having no friends is not necessarily a bad thing if that is your child's choice. However, being bullied is damaging and always needs to be addressed.

SOCIAL INTERACTIONS OUTSIDE OF SCHOOL (I.E. PLAY DATES AND PARTIES)

When children are in that 6 or 7–10 years age group, they are often invited to social events outside of school such as sleepovers and birthday parties. While these events are intended to be enjoyable, for many autistic children there are some difficulties associated with these events. Autistic children might be invited to a party by a school friend and be so happy and excited it triggers overload and meltdown or shutdown, even though the event is a positive one. Children can also become very anxious about exactly what is supposed to happen and what they are expected to do.

Something as apparently simple as selecting a gift for the friend who is having the party can become subject to perfectionism. By the ages of 7–10, some autistic children have picked up on differences between themselves and their peers and may be anxious about embarrassment if they get any social expectations 'wrong'. If you/your child is hosting a party, they may worry that nobody will turn up or that people won't have an enjoyable time.

A party is essentially a different sort of social setting to school, but often occurs with the same children who attend school. This means that one element of socialising, the relationship and communication with other children, is carried across into a different setting. The difference is the environment. Social events outside of school are important for autistic children to experience as they set them up for friendships in teenage years or young adult life. Being able to cope with unexpected changes in a social setting and being able to use the skills learnt in one social situation in another are great indicators for resilience.

Some signs your child is doing well with parties and social events outside of school include:

- Your child remains friends with children whose birthday party or other social event they have attended (although keep in mind that the other child may do something to end or change the friendship).

- Your child is more excited and positive than anxious and negative at the prospect of a party or sleepover.

- Your child expresses interest in the party or sleepover such as by giving suggestions on gifts for the birthday child or suggesting activities.

- If your child has attended a few parties or other social events, they are increasingly calmer about them.

- After attending a party or sleepover, your child expresses some enjoyment or excitement.

- Your child expresses the wish to have a party themselves.

ACTIVITIES TO BUILD RESILIENCE FOR SOCIAL EVENTS OUTSIDE OF SCHOOL

Activity 1 – Pre-party conversation

If you know the parents of the child whose party your child has been invited to and they know your child is autistic, you can hold a pre-party planning discussion. Get together, either at your house or at the friend's house, and encourage your child to ask any questions they have around the party which they might be anxious about. These could include questions such as:

- How many other children are coming?

- Who are they – have I met them before?

- What games and activities will be held? If I don't know them – can you show me the rules before the party?

- Here are some photos of me wearing things I like. Will one of these outfits be okay to wear? Have you decided what you are wearing? What is it?

- What food will be served? Is it okay to bring my own food, if I can't eat what you are having?

For children who do not use speech or children for whom the above would be too abstract, you can role play the party using objects such as Lego people, if they like Lego.

Activity 2 – Contributing to a party

If possible, speak to the parents of the child who is hosting the party and ask if your child can contribute an activity or game that they enjoy. This can give your child some agency in the social event, which is likely to make them feel less anxious and more engaged as it is something they are confident at and enjoys and they are sharing it with others. Parents will need to keep a keen eye on the activity to ensure other children are enjoying it and engaging with it, and it is not resulting in significant additional stress for your child. Your child will need to be skilled at sharing and turn-taking in order to manage the idea their game is not the only game at the party.

Activity 3 – An alternate party

Some autistic children do not cope with groups of excitable children so, while they may be excited to be invited to a party, the reality of it might be overwhelming and stressful. It is important to build social capabilities though. You can work up to social interactions outside of the home by hosting an alternate party. Plan a party with your child that is tailored to their own preferences. They may wish to invite one or two or a few friends and do an activity they enjoy. This may help build their social confidence and get them to a place where they might also enjoy a more traditional party at a friend's house:

> I wasn't often asked to go to parties and events by school friends. I was quite shy and didn't know what to say to start a friendship with people at my school. I knew people had birthday parties but I only went to one or two and didn't enjoy them at all.
>
> When I was about 8, I was really interested in the 19th century and all the class divisions. I read up all about kitchen maids and scullery maids. I even got a costume which I thought was like a maid in the 1800s. I got to organise a dinner for my family and decide what we ate. I had my one friend from school, Emily, and it was lovely. I didn't have to be overloaded by loud kids and music, but I had my own party based on my interest at the time. (Jeanne)

SLEEPOVERS

When children are in the later years of primary school, they are often invited to friend's houses for sleepovers, or friends want to come and visit them. While sleepovers are usually a positive thing, some autistic children struggle to be able to enjoy them. Anxiety around a range of potential issues can turn a planned sleepover into a very involved and challenging thing. Issues might include:

- *Food.* If your child is a selective eater or has allergies and intolerances, they might worry about what they are going to eat. Their concerns may not be unfounded as some parents dismiss dietary concerns.

- *Concerns around routine.* Things like different bedtimes, different evening rituals and activities, brushing your teeth, having a shower or going to bed at different times, can be anxiety-provoking for an autistic child.

- *Concerns around social interactions.* Things like worrying they won't have anything to talk about with their friend or concerns about their friend's siblings can be challenging. Siblings might be rude or pick on the autistic child and, even if they don't, the child can be anxious around this issue, especially if the siblings are older.

- *Feeling they are away from their familiar routine and home.* This can be especially true the first time your child goes on a sleepover.

- *Worrying they will upset their friend's family or do something 'wrong'.* This occasionally actually happens and to be in an unfamiliar setting with unfamiliar people when a social error of judgement or faux pas occurs can be incredibly stressful.

Sleepovers should be an enjoyable experience where children get to strengthen their friendships and get the opportunity to build their independence. Successfully navigating sleepovers is a great skill for resilience as it gets the child out of their comfort zone, but in what should be a supportive environment. It is a step away from parents and home. This can support a child's journey towards independent living:

When I was 9, I was invited to stay with a friend of mine from church. She was very quiet and introverted, and we liked talking about books. When I got to her house, though, I was quite anxious – it smelled odd, and her older brother had an injury on his toe and was showing it off. I have always been squeamish about looking at medical procedures and injuries. Then at dinner time they served lamb liver and mashed potatoes and peas. These were three foods I would never eat. Even my mum who tried to get me to eat things I didn't like wouldn't have presented any of those foods to me. I became really anxious as I didn't know her parents well, and I was scared they would try to force me to eat the food.

When my friend and I went to bed, she lent me a book with what I found really disturbing themes around disease and epidemics, and I didn't want to upset her by not reading it. When my parents came to collect me the next day, I was so relieved. Even though I liked my friend from church, I was never brave enough to stay at her home again... (Angela)

Some signs that your child is doing well with sleepovers include:

- They stay for the entire night, and you don't get called to pick them up.

- They are keen or willing to have another sleepover.

- They want to spend more time with the friend they had the sleepover with.

- They manage their emotions and stress levels well during the sleepover.

- When they return home, their stress levels are not significantly elevated or, if they are, this can be de-escalated relatively easily.

ACTIVITIES TO BUILD RESILIENCE FOR SLEEPOVERS
Activity 1 – Practice sleepover

Your child going to a strange house for a sleepover when they haven't done anything like that before can result in some issues particularly around anxiety. If possible, set up some practice sleepovers – your child could stay with an aunt or uncle they like or a close friend of the family they know well. They could even sleep in a tent in the backyard. Aim to make the whole experience fun and focus on how enjoyable and new it is. This also allows you to gauge your child's readiness for a sleepover, but because they are in a more supported place with people who can feed back any issues to you, it is a good first step. It should help build your child's confidence in themselves to have a 'real' sleepover with their friend.

Activity 2 – Detective game

If your child is anxious about an upcoming sleepover, you could give them an activity to do to help relieve their stress and engage with the experience of staying with their friend. The detective game involves making a list of things in your house that are familiar to your child. Then, ask your child to compare these things with the objects that they can see at their friend's house when they go on a sleepover. Items on the list could include the colour of kitchen cupboards, whether the floors are hard or carpet, what pets their friend has, if any. You could even ask your child to report back to you with their findings. This activity aims to refocus your child's thinking and anxiety into doing a fun activity which they can do with their friend as well.

GOING ON SCHOOL CAMP

When children are in the older years of primary school, they often get the opportunity to go on a school camp. For autistic kids, this can be a great opportunity to build resilience and independence, but it can also be very stressful. School camp may be the longest time a child has ever spent away from their parents' home. While parents can talk to teachers and support staff about any challenges that their child experiences, so that they can be aware of it, school camps can still be very difficult for autistic kids.

School camps can be fun, but they can also involve a lot of potentially stressful things, such as:

- dramatic change in routine

- being in a situation where children may share dorms and are expected to get changed in front of each other

- different food

- teachers being in a less formal role, which can be confusing

- blurring of the line between school and leisure time

- not knowing the 'script' or format for school camp.

Some ways to alleviate these issues can include things like parents liaising with the school and getting a very thorough itinerary to provide as a guide to their child. However, this can backfire when the itinerary unexpectedly changes. For autistic people, being given an itinerary that turns out to be inaccurate is often considerably worse than not having one at all. Therefore, children should be made aware that the plans may change and that is okay.

Months before camp, it is a good idea to set up a planning meeting with the school where you can raise any concerns and make plans for how to address those. In most countries, there are laws that address disability discrimination, and these give your child the right to attend school camp with reasonable supports. At the planning meeting, you could all decide that one of the teaching or support staff members on the camp is given specific responsibility to ensure your child is coping and to help address any issues that arise. Other reasonable supports are going for less time, taking their own food, being able to choose a friend to sleep near/next to, having a visual with them for bedtime and getting-up routines, and so on.

Being able to attend school camps and manage well is a factor in developing resilience as it takes your child out of their comfort zone and involves time away from home, which can help develop independence throughout the upcoming teen and adult years. Successfully attending a school camp also gives your child confidence, particularly if they were concerned before the camp.

Signs that your child is doing well at school camp include:

- They are open to the possibility of attending camp prior to it and not oppositional.

- Their anxiety levels before or after the camp are not extreme.

- Strategies that you use to address anxiety before and during the camp are effective.

- They want to talk to you about the camp when they return home – positives, negatives, amusing things, etc.

ACTIVITIES TO BUILD RESILIENCE ABOUT SCHOOL CAMP

Activity 1 – Setting up camp

If you have the time and funds, you can have a practice camp that mirrors what the school camp will be like, for example if school camp is camping in tents, have a couple of nights under canvas, with your child. If children at the camp are going to do a specific activity, do that with your child on your practice camp. Talk through any worries and concerns your child has.

Activity 2 – Camp planning and preparation

Be relaxed and confident when talking to your child about camp. Share stories about your camp if you have any. Talk about the things that are the same as home, such as your child will still go to sleep and get up, and things that are different. Make lists for what to pack, practise packing and unpacking. Talk about what your child should do if they are briefly unhappy or anxious, who they can go to for support, or what can do to feel better. Suggest they use strategies that they already have and already use by giving examples of these. Talk about the transient nature of home sickness and the fun that can be had at camp:

> When I was 9, my class at school went on a school camp to Canberra. I sort of liked the idea of going on camp before I went, but when I got on the bus, I got really anxious about being away from home and being with my classmates for whole days. A couple of the boys in my class were really nasty bullies, and they always took the opportunity to give me a hard time. I spent the whole bus trip being really anxious. We were going away for three days, but it seemed an eternity.
>
> I didn't know at the time, but my dad had talked to my teacher because he thought I might have some issues, so, when we got to where we were staying, my teacher came up and talked to me. She wasn't obvious or anything, but she was just there for the whole trip. If I had a hard time, my teacher would just take me aside, and we would talk about it. And it was hard for bullies to harass me because my teacher had her eye on me pretty much the whole time we were away and would somehow just turn up at the hint of any aggression from others. It meant I actually enjoyed a lot of the camp. And when we got back home, I was the most engaged and attentive kid in the class, because I was so grateful to my teacher. (Jake)

DEALING WITH MAJOR DISAPPOINTMENT

Like failure and making mistakes, disappointment is an inevitable part of life. It isn't pleasant but for autistic children it can be quite traumatic. Autistic children are often perfectionists who try to avoid every kind of failure or setback. Disappointment is even worse than failure in many ways, because it tends to happen externally to the child. It is usually not something that can be controlled. Autistic children often find change incredibly difficult. Disappointment is a change of sorts, a deviation from that which was expected. Some parents might think that their child is overreacting when they have a meltdown related to something being cancelled (or whatever). They might even think that the meltdown is a tantrum intended to manipulate the situation in the child's favour. Generally this isn't the case. The extreme reaction to an apparently minor disappointment is more likely to be related to the stress of having the nice future your child has planned in their mind suddenly disappearing and being replaced with uncertainty. You can teach your child to better manage disappointment.

Signs that your child is managing disappointment well include:

- Decreasing extreme reactions to disappointments.

- Less anxiety around upcoming events (e.g. continually seeking reassurance around events and activities, checking the time, etc.)

- Increasing ability to assimilate disappointments when they occur.

ACTIVITIES TO SUPPORT YOUR CHILD TO RESILIENTLY MANAGE DISAPPOINTMENT

Activity 1 – The roadmap

This activity involves considering your child's need for certainty. For many autistic people, potential changes are managed through having a mental map of the future. When they know that something will happen, they add it to their 'roadmap' and it makes them feel less anxious. A disappointment, something being cancelled or even not getting the grade they expected for a school assignment can throw this mental roadmap out of kilter. The job for parents is to work with their child to create a more flexible roadmap that can change with events. Discuss with your child what might happen and what they expect to happen but which may also not occur. You can do this using visuals, role plays, written documents or conversation.

If you use an actual roadmap for this, you can show how turning left instead of right does not prevent you from getting to your destination, it just takes you through a variety of different twists and turns.

Activity 2 – Preparation

One of the things that autistic children struggle with is things coming out of left field – unexpected events and disappointment often fit that. Work through expectations and the fact that things don't always go according to plan with your child. Emphasise the concept that unexpected events and disappointments are part of life and are perfectly okay. You can work through contingencies – what do you do if something your child has planned and is looking forward to does not eventuate?

> When I was 9, I really wanted to learn piano. My parents told me they were going to pay for lessons, and I was really excited. My dad was a farmer, and so our family finances were always pretty unpredictable. About two weeks before my piano lessons were meant to start, my dad announced we were having a bad year, and we couldn't afford piano lessons. I was devastated. I was angry with my dad for about six months. I thought it was completely unfair, especially as I had done a bunch of research about pieces of music for the piano and imagined myself playing at concerts. I felt like my dream had been shattered. I think one of the worst things was that nobody had told me the piano lessons might be cancelled, so it was a total surprise, and I had to work though that uncertain event in my mind. If someone had said, 'The lessons are conditional on how our financial situation is going,' it would have been much easier for me to accept. (Jade)

LOSING A GAME

Autistic children can often be quite competitive at games and find it hard when someone other than them wins. Some people address this by playing cooperative games, which is a great idea. However, the concept of graciously losing at a game extends beyond childhood. A lot of situations in adult life require the ability to lose well: in study when students are graded or in employment when applying for a job in the competitive labour market. Adult life has a lot of situations where being able to accept 'defeat' and not become too fixated on or bitter about the loss is a very useful resilience skill and it may be best learnt in childhood.

It is important to know when to introduce competitive games and the concept of a 'good loser' to children, as all children are different and their maturity and understanding of the world beyond their experience can vary dramatically even at the same age. Use your judgement based on how your child has reacted in the past to being 'beaten' in games or how they respond to arguments and competition with siblings or peers. Introducing competitive games can start on a very small scale with a game between parents and the autistic child. If your child has siblings and they play well together, it can help to have siblings playing as well, but if there is antagonism between siblings start out with the game between you and your child.

Some autistic children can become highly anxious when presented with the possibility of a game as they worry they won't win. Uncertainty can also be stressful for autistic people and games tend to involve a lot of uncertainty, which could be why many people enjoy playing them.

Not only can a child be an ungracious loser, they might also be an ungracious winner, delighting in beating family members or friends at a game or activity. This can be hard for friends and siblings to respond to and may have people passing judgement on your child. Many autistic children can be quite competitive and winning is very important to them. This can be particularly true for kids who don't 'win' much in life outside of games. They may be unaware that their poor winning behaviour might be upsetting to their friends or siblings. For some autistic children, a parent or other trusted adult pointing out to them the impact their gloating might have on others is enough. Contrary to stereotypes, autistic people are often very thoughtful and considerate, but they may need some prompting to understand the impact of their behaviour on others.

Difficulties with losing and competitive tasks can be related to a variety of other issues that might seem unrelated. These include things like perfectionism, a response to bullying or poor self-esteem, a lack of feeling safe and supported or a perceived need to gain approval from parents.

> **Signs that your child is managing winning and losing well include:**
>
> - Less anxiety around playing games.
>
> - Decreasing or no extreme responses to losing or winning.
>
> - Your child takes as much or more interest and enjoyment from actually playing the game as from winning the game.

ACTIVITIES TO BUILD RESILIENCE WITH LOSING

Activity 1 – Understanding the reason for games

Talk to your child about what games are: that they are supposed to be enjoyable and sometimes educational; that winning or losing is simply part of the game and doesn't go any further than that. If you lose at Monopoly, for example, you are not a 'loser' in life. You can even create a new game with assistance from your child and encourage them to think about what the purpose of the game is.

Activity 2 – Thinking about control

Difficulties responding to losing games can stem from a lack of a sense of control and agency. Winning a game helps the child to feel they are in control and literally 'winning'. Children who feel insecure within society or the family may focus on winning to give them confidence. Children who struggle with sibling rivalry may also focus on winning when playing games with their sibling(s). For parents, this competitive behaviour, especially when it is within the family, can be very difficult to manage, especially if more than one sibling has the same need to 'win'.

This activity is a thinking one and involves parents thinking about issues around control and dominance and considering whether this is a problem in their family. Following on from that thinking and analysis, it can help to provide a greater sense of control to your child or children where possible. This might mean giving them some responsibility with a task or giving them the opportunity to select an activity and be involved with its planning and delivery, as much as possible:

When I was a young boy, I used to play games with my sister, who is younger than me. I hated her winning. It got to almost being an obsession. I would beat her at everything. Very occasionally, she would win at something and I would be mean to her for days. I guess I wanted to be in control. Now, I am quite surprised she would play me at any game knowing that I would not only win, but I would 'terminate with extreme prejudice' her efforts at the game if I got the chance. I have stayed competitive my whole life since then, including with board games. I get the feeling that everyone else sees games as fun but I find it hard to not be very serious and need to win. (Nathan)

RESPONDING RESILIENTLY TO BULLYING

Sadly, bullying is all too common in schools, and autistic kids are often on the receiving end of unwanted aggression and cruelty from fellow students. Bullying can occur in many settings, in the physical environment of school but also online. Cyberbullying is particularly dangerous as it can mean that the child does not even feel safe at home. There is no doubt as to the impact of any kind of bullying, but this is particularly pronounced when directed towards impressionable children. It can result in low self-esteem, self-hatred and things like post-traumatic stress disorder, depression, self-harm and suicide. Bullying is never okay and should not be tolerated or ignored in any setting. Autistic children are likely to have social anxiety and difficulties being themselves at school. Bullying compounds this and can lead to a lifetime of self-doubt and self-hatred. Autistic people have a number of issues to contend with that can't be changed. Bullying is an additional problem that is largely preventable.

There are several issues that make bullying in childhood difficult to address. These include:

- *Lack of knowledge that it is occurring.* Many parents are unaware that their child is being bullied and many autistic children do not realise they need to tell someone what is going on.

- *Invalidation or denial by school staff members.* Some autistic children complain of bullying to an adult only to have their concerns dismissed or ignored. Sometimes, they or their parents are given largely unhelpful advice such as, 'You wouldn't be bullied if you were more resilient.' While that statement is essentially true, it doesn't help a lot. First, it is blaming the victim. It can be viewed as saying, 'You need to change your own behaviour in order to stop the bully being aggressive to you.' It is also impossible to acquire resilience overnight. It is a bit like saying to the child, 'If you grew 10 cm taller overnight, you wouldn't be bullied.' That is also probably true but impossible. Other dismissive comments can include statements like, 'Just keep away from the bully.' A school yard is not a very big place and bullies tend to find their victims quite easily. This is also another example of victim-blaming.

- *Autistic children can be very trusting, even at older ages.* This can be exploited by bullies, who will often ask the child to do something under the guise of friendship or inclusion. The autistic child – keen to make friends – will do some publicly embarrassing thing and be surprised when the apparent friendship with the bully results in them being ridiculed by the other children. This sort of bullying can occur on many occasions with the autistic child desperate to find approval.

- *Autistic children can sometimes be bullies.* In some instances, autistic children can themselves become bullies in order to be accepted by their peers.

- *Sometimes, autistic children can be disciplined for taking matters into their own hands and fighting back.* Because autistic children tend to operate on one level and not consider things like who is watching when they fight back, they can be disciplined when the bully themselves gets away with their behaviour.

- *Bullying is not an inevitable result of autistic children's social skills.* It is important to note that bullying should not be seen as an inevitable result of autistic kids' apparently less-developed social skills. In the bully–victim relationship, it might be more accurate to see the person with the lower level of social skills as the bully.

Bullying is a significant and complex issue often requiring many strategies and approaches to address it. Autistic children need protecting and they need to understand what they can do to strengthen their own ability to stay safe and report bullying behaviour. Strategies to address bullying also need to address the behaviour of the bully, given that is the key factor in the issue. Evidence shows that school bullies – and particularly boys – have poor outcomes as adults including higher rates of unemployment, low school attainment, social exclusion and imprisonment. While it may be hard to sympathise with bullies, improving outcomes for them also benefits society through things like less criminal behaviour.

If your child is being bullied, it is important that you know about it, that you report it to the school or place where it is occurring and that you help your child to work through the issues the bullying has caused. Bullying is sustained or ongoing harassment, intimidation and social exclusion as well as physical or verbal aggression. Often, the bullying of autistics is more subtle than overt.

Signs that your child is addressing issues around bullying well include:

- That your child can – either now or over time, through prompting – understand what is bullying behaviour and what they need to do to help address it.

- Your child is able to tell you or a staff member at school about the bullying.

- That on some level, your child is able to work with you or a mental health or autism professional to share what emotional issues the bullying has caused.

- Your child knows on some level that they are valued and cared for.

I am now 44 years old and finished school almost 30 years ago. I was not diagnosed as being on the autism spectrum until I was in my 30s, and the appropriate diagnosis wasn't even available until several years after I finished school.

I absolutely hated school. The academic side of it was fine. I enjoyed maths, English and art, but the social side was terrible, I was the target of bullies from about age 8 to 18. At high school, I was easily the least popular child there. On the school bus, at lunchtime and recess and then the school bus home again, I was taunted, physically assaulted and insulted. The weekend was my only reprieve from this almost constant aggression, and I am very glad that the internet wasn't around when I was a kid, because I probably would have experienced cyberbullying as well if it was.

The impact of 10 years of people telling me every day what a terrible person I was and backing that up with different forms of violence, made my adult life very challenging. My self-esteem even now is quite poor, and I am anxious meeting people as I think they will bully and hate me. The other day, I was on a bus, and all the school kids got on. I was incredibly anxious and thought they were going to victimise me. That is almost 30 years after I last went to school. Bullying is a terrible thing, and I wouldn't wish it on anybody. (Jenny)

ACTIVITIES TO HELP YOUR CHILD RESPOND RESILIENTLY TO BULLYING

Activity 1 – Talking about positive and negative 'friendship'

Write down on cards some of the things that your child's peers might do, some of them representing genuine friendship and some representing bullying. Talk to your child about each of these and whether they are 'good friendship' or bullying. It can be hard to communicate social behaviour to autistic children verbally and through memories or statements. To address this, you could ask your child if they can give an example of one of the actions on the cards occurring and whether it was 'good' or 'bad'. This can be a basis for discussions and, if your child comes home and tells you about an instance of bullying, you can go back to the cards and talk through it.

Another way to look at this is through watching TV or videos together and discussing or analysing the behaviours of the children and/or adults. Understanding the intent of people is surprisingly difficult for many autistic children, so they use knowledge of previous examples to try and work out if people are being kind or not. This is problematic because, if the previous example was a bit different, it can be hard for an autistic child to generalise that to the new situation.

Activity 2 – Separating negative statements

In children, bullying often takes the form of name calling and insults. These can be incredibly hurtful and have an impact on an autistic child's sense of self-worth from a very young age. Teasing and name-calling might seem a mild form of aggression, but it can be insidious and have an impact on a person's adult life for many years. Explain to your child the evolving nature of language so they can understand some of the insults that they hear.

Work with your child to develop a list or positive attributes they have. Make it fun and get them to 'own' their positive qualities, by telling you about them. If your child, or you, enjoys art you could draw characters representing the positive qualities your child has identified. Tell your child that these qualities are part of them and whatever any bully tells them, the positive qualities are still there. If your child reports an instance of bullying, help them regain their own sense of self-worth by looking at or thinking about their positive qualities. You can even get them to do a drawing representing their positive qualities in overcoming the negative words from the bully.

GOING TO RESTAURANTS AND CAFÉS

Going out to a restaurant or café for coffee or a meal is something most people find enjoyable and can be a good way for parents to catch up with other parents they are friends with. For an autistic child, a meal out can be quite different from one at home. There are many different cafés and restaurants in many cities and towns; each one is different and each serves different sorts of food or different variations of the same dish. This is often challenging for autistic children, who may prefer routine at mealtimes. Being out of home in a strange environment can be difficult too, and is often compounded by strange smells, loud conversations or music in the café, people walking around unpredictably and different expectations of behaviour.

Going out might be enjoyable for the parent but some children can really struggle. If they find it difficult to articulate and express emotion or sensory distress, the first anyone knows of the autistic child's distress is when they have a meltdown. The world is not as autism-confident as it should be and a child's meltdown may be seen as a tantrum or some other form of poor behaviour. This can set up anxiety and fear around going out, which can result in the child not wanting or being able to go out for meals at all.

This does not have to be the reality for you and your child, though. Managing expectations and anxiety around eating out can help a lot. The attitude you have towards going out can be important, too. If it is viewed as a 'big deal' and you build it up as a big occasion, for some children this will just make them worry more and be concerned about 'what if I do it wrong?' If children go to restaurants and cafés from a young age and it is simply part of the daily routine, this can address some of the issues around anxiety at the different setting:

> My parents have always taken us out to eat at other people's houses, to picnics and to cafés and restaurants. It was always just a part of life. I did need teaching not to say things that other people took as rudeness. I apparently, infamously (in our family), offended a great aunt in London when I was about 6 or so by saying, 'Your chicken tasted much nicer than it looked.' (Emma)

Another issue around eating out is the food served. If a child has food aversions and allergies/intolerances, eating out can be very difficult. Often, a familiar dish will be called something different at a restaurant, although that can represent a positive opportunity to introduce your child to food in different places. One thing many parents of autistic and non-autistic children do is go to the same restaurant or group of restaurants so the initial visit may be anxiety-provoking but subsequent visits are more likely to be familiar and enjoyable.

Being able to eat out, try new foods or determine which food is acceptable and spend time in different environments with different 'rules' and expectations are all great resilience and independence skills that will support autistic children in later life:

> My parents were pretty unconventional, which was a good thing. My dad's family owned hotels since long before I was born. Going out for dinner was a bit of a special treat, and it has been part of my life for as long as I remember. I was a bit atypical for an Aspie as I would try any new food as a kid. When I was about 11, we went to an Indian restaurant, and I absolutely loved the spicy food. I thought it was like

making lunch more exciting. I wanted to go to that Indian restaurant all the time! One day, my dad drove me into town and gave me some money and said I could dine in the restaurant all by myself (but he was up the other end of the restaurant room, just in case anything unexpected happened). So, I had the money and I looked at the menu and decided what I wanted and ordered it. When I was finished, I paid the waiter and met my dad on the way out. I think my dad must have talked to the staff and told them I would be there. It was just the best thing. I felt so grown up and I had done something most 11-year-olds don't get to do – ordered off a menu by myself and paid for the meal like I had earned the money by working. (Angela)

How to know that your child is managing going to restaurants and cafés well:

- They are willing or enthusiastic to eat out.

- They are not overly anxious at the prospect of eating out, and if they are, their anxiety lessens when and after they go to the restaurant.

- They express a preference for a café or restaurant and ask to go there.

ACTIVITIES TO BUILD RESILIENCE AROUND GOING TO RESTAURANTS AND CAFÉS
Activity 1 – Restaurant game

With your child, at home, role play a restaurant. Your child can play whatever part they like: proprietor, chef, waiting staff, customer. Work out a menu of things that your child would like to eat and go through all the different roles. You can even get your child to serve some actual food. Talk about how eating out can be enjoyable and, while it is a bit special, it is also something people do all the time. You can get your child to name their restaurant and what decor they would have, anything which engages and empowers them around restaurant eating.

Activity 2 – Restaurant rules

With your child, create a video of how to manage in a café or restaurant. Focus on moving around safely, ordering food/drink and paying before leaving. Watch the video together to learn the rules and then take the video with you on a café visit. Play each section and then let your child do that part. Celebrate all the steps that have been achieved successfully.

CHAPTER 7

FAILING SUCCESSFULLY

WHY FAILING WELL IS A VITAL SKILL

Being able to fail well is an essential life skill for every single person. Not being traumatised by making a mistake but instead acknowledging it and moving on is a very useful strategy for being able to take on challenges, try new things and learn important lessons. Being able to fail successfully is a great skill that translates across all elements of life. Successful failing is a core element of building resilience and 'bouncing back' from setbacks. Failing successfully is a skill that autistic children can learn and that will help them build their resilience and independence.

Most people do not enjoy failure. It is frustrating, disappointing and stressful. For autistic people, particularly children, failure can be highly traumatic and lead to feelings of inadequacy and self-criticism. Combined with the negative messaging they may receive around their capability, failing can result in autistic children giving up before they even start. Failure and mistakes can also become caught up with anxiety and fear of change. Autistic children can be so worried about getting something wrong that it heightens their anxiety around the task, sometimes leading to failure, which further compounds their anxiety and may result in them refusing to try again. Fear of failure can work against resilience and independence, as children may be unwilling to take on new tasks for fear of failing. Perfectionism and performance anxiety can be a risk factor around failing successfully.

Resilience can be viewed in a sense as the antithesis to fear of failure. To take on a new task or challenge in an effort to build resilience requires some understanding that failure is not 'the end of the world' in most cases. If a child is too anxious about failing to take on an activity or task, then it will be harder for them to build their resilience and independence. So, understanding issues around mistakes and failure is at the heart of supporting autistic children to become more resilient.

Parents can play a significant part in lessening the fear of failure and support their children to take on new challenges.

FAILURE AND MISTAKES ARE INEVITABLE

There is a phrase: 'to err is human'. Every single one of us will make mistakes and fail, often many times over. Autistic people can be highly anxious about making a mistake but one is inevitably going to occur at some point. It is important to help children understand that they will make mistakes but that it is okay.

There is a scale of magnitude for errors and failure. How significant the error is may determine the response. If your child forgets a school book, that is not really a significant error, so the response would be to support your child to understand that it's not a big deal and maybe work on some strategies with them to ensure they remembers their book in future and what to do in the moment. However, physical violence against a sibling or peer is a mistake with more complex consequences and will need to be handled differently. This kind of mistake requires discussion around consequences and an understanding of what the factors were which led up to the incident occurring. In these situations, children can become overwhelmed with remorse, which they may turn inward on themselves or alternatively react defiantly to discipline or any directions or requests for them to apologise. As such, understanding the nature and impact of the error drives how you will need to work with your child to turn it into a learning experience. Don't forget that behaviours which occur due to sympathetic nervous system responses require completely different responses than behaviours over which the child has some control.

MAKING FAILURE USEFUL

Using the example above around your child hitting another child, there may be responses to this mistake from the parent(s) and from the school. The child can respond to the discipline and feel guilty around the event and dwell on it. They may become highly anxious about making mistakes and incurring parental or school discipline. This can be very unhelpful. Unless they understand the reason for the discipline and how to address the issue, in this case aggression, they may not actually take any useful lessons from the experience and it could just contribute to their anxiety or antagonism around school and interacting with fellow students and teachers, which may well be significant already.

Instead of dwelling on the event, it is much better for parents to move from guilt and discipline and into the constructive space of successful failure. Parents can work through what went wrong, why it happened and how their child can manage similar situations in the future. Social Stories™ or role playing can be used to assist with the discussion. It needs to be constructive and focused on building understanding of what went wrong and why, and how to avoid it happening again. Parents need to avoid blaming, but their child does need to know that they made an error which had consequences and that they can learn from this for the future.

For younger children and those who have difficulties with cognition or understanding consequences, this message may need to be simplified. Following the discussion, instead of the child feeling a whole lot of nebulous anxiety and guilt or defiance, they will hopefully learn a constructive lesson from their mistake, which will enable them to not make the same mistake again. Children require teaching how to behave and how to recognise, respond and manage their feelings and emotions, in the same way that they require teaching to ride a bike or read a book.

THE VALUE OF SUCCESSFUL FAILURE IN CHILDHOOD

One feature of today's society is the strong focus on the welfare of children and ensuring they have an enjoyable and positive journey through life. There is absolutely nothing wrong with this philosophy. In fact, this can be a great foundation for parenting and teaching children. While positive experiences and growth and having a supportive and positive life are great for children, it is important for parents and educators to understand that it is not possible, or advisable, to shield a child from making any errors. If this happens, the first time a young adult fails, for example by not getting a job that they have applied for, they will be devastated. Helping children build resilience around errors and failure when they are young is very useful for them as they grow up.

The world can be a difficult and invalidating place. For autistic children, these difficulties can be more evident than in typically developing children. If you think back to the young man in the introduction to this book who had significant issues with independence, two things seem to have been at play in creating his challenges with living independently. The first was a focus on deficits rather than the strengths of autistic children and adults. When the young man was diagnosed at 7 years old, one can only imagine what his parents were told by clinicians, what they saw in the media and what peers and relatives told them about autism. There was probably a strong focus on how limiting autism is, how raising autistic children was incredibly hard, maybe even how having an autistic child was somehow unfair. The sorts of messaging in the world can be very negative and parents can understandably lower the bar for their autistic child based on these sorts of messages. Expectations of the child's ability to learn and achieve can be very low indeed.

For the young man in the introduction to this book, one of the main challenges in his formative years seems to have been extreme parental anxiety. Related to this anxiety is the idea of wanting your child to have an entirely positive life free from setbacks and challenges.

Experiencing setbacks, disappointments, mistakes and challenges that haven't gone according to plan, as well as argument and conflict are all part of human development. Autistic children need to have these sorts of experiences in order to build their capacity to deal with similar issues in adult life. If they do not, they may become like the young man in the introduction to this book.

WHAT DOES SUCCESSFUL FAILURE LOOK LIKE IN AUTISTIC KIDS?

Learning to fail successfully is usually an incremental process. Like resilience more broadly, it is good to start thinking about strengthening your child's ability to handle setbacks and failure as early as you can.

Two to six years

At the ages of 2–6 years, failing successfully might include being able to:

- Restart an activity (e.g. art, craft or a game) that has not worked out.

- Reach their usual resting emotional state sooner after frustration from losing a game or making a mistake, or in increasingly lower timeframes.

- Be able on some level to work through or discuss the failure or setback with a parent.

- Apologise, with some prompting if required, after poor behaviour or interpersonal issues where they make the wrong choice.

- Demonstrate on some level that they have learnt from the experience over coming days/weeks/months.

Seven to ten years

At the ages of 7–10 years, failing successfully might include being able to:

- Work through or discuss the failure or setback with a parent or trusted adult.

- Listen to constructive criticism without meltdown, shutdown or extreme reactions.

- Understand, independently or with some prompting, why they made a mistake.

- Understand, independently or with some prompting, what they can learn from their mistake.

- Apologise, with some prompting if required, after poor behaviour or interpersonal issues where they make the wrong choice and work on a way to address the behaviour in the future.

- Assimilate and take on board new behaviours or thinking based on understanding the reasons for the mistake or failure.

CHALLENGES FOR AUTISTIC CHILDREN AROUND FAILING

Failure and mistakes happen for all people at all ages. Most typically developing children struggle with mistakes, failure and setbacks, too. It is not an experience unique to autistics. However, autistic children may have some additional challenges around failing, including:

- Failing may compound anxiety and may lead to the child not attempting the task they failed at a second time.

- Failing may feed insecurity and self-doubt leading to a negative self-perception and a lack of confidence in attempting new activities or the activity the child failed at. That can be a significant risk factor for lacking resilience and independence.

- Failing may coincide with perfectionism. Perfectionism can cause a kind of action paralysis, which means that the child will not do anything – or finish tasks – unless they consider them to be perfect. For a perfectionist, failure may be their biggest fear. So, failure can feed into perfectionism and vice versa.

- Autistic children may try to avoid failure or mistakes at any cost, which can stop any work on building their resilience.

IMPACTS OF NOT DOING FAILURE WELL

Not being able to successfully manage failure or making mistakes can have a range of challenges and difficulties associated with it, including increasing the risks to well-being and mental illness.

In autistic children and teens, not being able to manage failure and mistakes can mean:

- an inability to take on any new tasks or activities or to revisit things that have been unsuccessful in the past

- feeling the need to be proficient at a task immediately; if this does not occur, the child may abandon the task

- increased perfectionism and anxiety

- avoiding social situations due to previous faux pas

- limited or no understanding of the consequences of behaviour

- an inability to respect and/or set limits and boundaries

- school refusal, not wanting to see people who have witnessed errors or poor behaviour, difficulties maintaining friendships

- self-doubt, insecurity.

In adult life, an inability to manage failure and mistakes can result in:

- difficulty acquiring independent living skills

- fear of engaging socially

- withdrawal, which may include gaming/internet addiction

- heightened anxiety

- low educational attainment level

- unemployment, being unable to join the workforce

- in some cases, a lack of being able to fail well may compound existing issues or contribute to mental health conditions.

It should be noted that factors other than difficulty failing, including external factors, can also result in or contribute to these issues.

HOW TO TEACH AUTISTIC CHILDREN TO FAIL SUCCESSFULLY

Failure and mistakes are best viewed as an opportunity to learn lessons and move on.

A parent's attitude and response to failure can strongly influence how a child feels about making mistakes and failing. Where the negative aspect of a failure or mistake is emphasised by parents and the prevailing attitudes are those of blame, recrimination and regret, a child is more likely to cope poorly with failure. Even if the parent is supportive and/or does not apportion blame, but places a lot of emphasis on the failure itself rather than how the mistake can become a useful learning experience, autistic children can still struggle.

Attitudes to failure can be viewed either from a past-focused or future-focused approach. When you are past-focused, you are looking back to the mistake: why the child did the wrong thing, what the consequences were, and so on. For most people, including non-autistic people, this approach often makes it hard to move on from the error. When you approach the mistake from a future-focused position, it can be used as the basis of learning lessons and strategies for the future. Acknowledge what happened and allow your child to apologise or make reparations if that is required. Then shift the focus to look forward from the mistake into the future. The mistake is not something to dwell on but something to learn from. This can help enable your child to fail successfully and start to learn to make adversity their teacher.

TALKING TO YOUR CHILD ABOUT SUCCESSFUL FAILURE

If your child fails at something or makes a mistake, talk about why it happened and how they can address the issue in the future. Keep blame out of the conversation as much as possible, both your own blame and your child's self-admonishment. You can tailor your message depending on your child's age, personality, learning style and approach, and level of cognitive capacity. Don't forget that most mistakes happen because the child is not yet skilled enough to know what to do, or how to manage the situation.

Some practical ways to help your child learn to fail successfully include:

- *Validating your child.* When a child has behaved poorly or acted without thinking, it is very easy to tell them what they have done wrong and focus on the behaviour or error. This is not necessarily a problem in itself, but they also need validation from parents in order to turn the messaging around their mistake into something that helps them move forward and avoid that mistake in the future. If your messaging is all blame and discipline and no validation, it may result in self-hatred and your child thinking they are somehow 'bad'. These attitudes are in fact counterproductive in terms of your child's resilience journey. Autistic children particularly can be very prone to this kind of all or nothing response to discipline. It is important for them to know that you are displeased with the error they made but not with them *per se.*

- *Don't shame or belittle kids.* Autistic kids are often in tune with emotions of others and may have a lot of self-doubt, identity issues and/or self-hatred. If a parent or trusted adult belittles or shames a child, it is not constructive or helpful, and may well result in the child being frightened of failure or even afraid of their parent.

- *Autistic children can become very caught up in guilt and regret and how they are doing things 'wrong'.* Even if their parent is supportive and positive, they may beat themselves up emotionally over and over again following a failure. In this instance, parents can help their child unpack the error and how the consequences are not as bad as their child thinks. Working on other psychological issues can also be of assistance. Anxiety and perfectionism frequently drive dwelling on errors so interventions to assist with these issues can help.

- *Communicating differences.* It is important to note that actions or behaviour seen as 'mistakes' by schools, and society more broadly, can often be the result of misunderstandings between autistic and non-autistic styles of communication. An autistic child might do something 'wrong' in response to a genuine concern or a misunderstanding. Some autistic children can go through school being seen as rebellious or difficult when, in fact, that was not their intent. Sometimes, misinterpretation of behaviours can even lead to an autistic child taking on a persona of disobedience simply because that is how they are viewed.

- *Providing reassurance.* Helping your child know what to do if the situation occurs again in the future.

EXERCISE – MISINTERPRETATIONS OF BEHAVIOUR

Imagine you are a 5-year-old autistic girl. You started school recently. One of the first classes you had was to learn letters and handwriting. The teacher wrote in beautiful cursive script, and the typed letters you saw on the computer screen were perfect, too. You know your letters and could read before starting school but you never tried to write.

After showing you her beautiful handwriting and the typed letters, your teacher gives all the students a pencil and pad of paper. You are really happy, thinking you will make beautiful letters like the teacher did. But when you hold the pencil, it feels wrong. You want to ask the teacher to help, but she is talking to other children. You try to draw an 'A' with the pencil, and it looks awful. You are really anxious, but you try to draw a 'B' – maybe it is just As you can't draw. But the same thing happens. You feel very anxious and start crying. The teacher comes over and asks what's wrong, but you are so stressed you can't tell her. In your mind, you will never be able to write. Nobody told you that it was a skill you needed to practise. The teacher puts her hand on your shoulder without asking if it is okay to do so. You run out of the classroom and hide in the playground. The school calls your mum. You don't understand what you have done wrong. You ask your mum if you will ever be able to write. She is puzzled, and you don't get an answer. You were looking forward to going to school, but now you are anxious about going back:

- What did the teacher need to know to be able to teach this student more effectively?

- What might the student have thought in response to the reaction from the school (calling the mother, etc.)?

- How could you assist the student to learn to write when she returns to school?

Now, think about your current responses to your child's mistakes and how they react currently to situations where they know that they have made a mistake or failed at something.

BUILDING SELF-ESTEEM AND SELF-CONFIDENCE FOR AUTISTIC CHILDREN

Children who have self-confidence and good self-esteem are often more confident in how they approach life and may be less likely to be thrown by a mistake or setback. As you support and encourage your child's resilience, they are likely to be able to recover from making a mistake or failing at something more easily. Self-confidence, self-esteem, resilience and successful falling can all be seen as part of a positive dynamic. The elements can feed into each other and strengthen your child's ability to manage setbacks, challenges, change and adversity. A great starting point is to build your child's level of self-esteem.

The raisingchildren.net.au website defines self-esteem in young children as:

> Self-esteem is about liking yourself and who you are. This doesn't mean being overconfident – just believing in yourself and knowing what you do well.
>
> For children, self-esteem comes from knowing that you're loved and that you belong to a family that values you. It also comes from being praised and encouraged for the things that are important to you, and from feeling confident about the future.[1]

WHAT DOES SELF-ESTEEM LOOK LIKE?

For autistic children, self-esteem may look a little different from self-esteem in typically developing children. Given the challenges that many autistic children face, what a parent needs to know about supporting and promoting their self-esteem may be different to parents of typically developing children.

The activities in this book form part of building your child's level of self-esteem along with resilience. Other actions that parents can take to boost self-esteem include:

- making sure they feel included in the family

- validating and supporting them – being 'in their corner', especially in difficult times

- emphasising their strengths and skills and avoiding focus on errors and deficits

---

1   Source: http://raisingchildren.net.au/articles/self-esteem.html (accessed 31 January 2017).

- loving them in a way that makes sense to them; for example, if your child dislikes hugs or physical contact, find another way to demonstrate that you love them, preferably one they initiate

- celebrating their achievements

- maintaining their sense of a place of safety throughout their childhood and as they grow older

- understanding them and not punishing them for things that are perceived as poor behaviour but are instinctive reactions

- setting boundaries and limits that support them to build their skills around interacting with others and negotiating the social world

- taking an interest in their interests.

CHALLENGES TO SELF-ESTEEM FOR AUTISTIC CHILDREN

Challenges to self-esteem are often similar to the challenges or risk factors around resilience. Invalidation and having their concerns dismissed are often significant challenges to self-esteem for autistic children and adults. Adult role models focusing only on deficits and problems can also be a threat to self-esteem. Basically, many of the things that pose a threat to resilience and independence for autistic children also pose a threat to self-esteem. In many cases, as self-esteem retreats so, too, does resilience.

Having their natural way of being and experiencing the world invalidated can also damage the self-esteem of autistic children. For example, when an autistic child says that it is noisy in their classroom and their teacher says that it is not, because the teacher's hearing is less sensitive than the child's, this invalidates the child's experience. Autistic children are invalidated more frequently when their sensory strengths and difficulties are unknown to the adults around them. For this reason, it is important to work with your child to develop a comprehensive sensory overview of them that incorporates strategies to enable them to learn in school and participate comfortably and confidently in family life.

Teaching your autistic child to self-advocate is one of the best ways to ensure that their self-esteem is resilient when challenged by people who do not understand them or their autism. Self-advocacy is the ability to say what you need in order to be able to do something or access a particular place or activity. Some examples of self-advocacy by children are given below:

I need to wear my sunglasses in assembly because the lights in the hall hurt my eyes.

I get agitated by the sun, so if it is hot, I need to spend playtime in a cooler area.

I have really sensitive hearing, so I can hear the class next door. When I am working, I will be more engaged if I can wear my headphones.

WHAT DOES SELF-ESTEEM LOOK LIKE IN DIFFERENT AGE GROUPS?

Children at two to six years

> **Signs that young children have some self-esteem include:**
>
> - They talk about themselves in a positive way some or most of the time.
>
> - They demonstrate love or affection for you and other family members in their own way.
>
> - The way your child talks about other people, pets, friends – real and imaginary – is largely positive.
>
> - Your child can ask for or initiate an activity which they enjoy.
>
> - Your child does not frequently describe themselves in negative terms.

Children at seven to ten years

Signs that children from 7–10 years have some self-esteem include:

- Friends or peers your child mixes with treat your child and themselves with respect.

- Your child demonstrates affection to family members in whichever way they demonstrate their affection.

- Your child talks about themselves in mostly positive terms.

- Your child's confidence to take on new activities or more difficult tasks is increasing.

- Your child can speak about an interest or passion to you or others.

- Your child's passionate/special interests are affirming or at least not destructive and negative.

PROTECTIVE FACTORS FOR SELF-ESTEEM

Protective factors for self-esteem are similar to those for resilience. The basis of self-esteem and resilience for autistic children, and all children, is the place of safety. A family that supports the child as they develop and loves and respects them as they are is absolutely crucial. A family does not need to be made up of any one configuration and can include one parent, two parents or an extended group and comprise any gender(s), it can be a birth family, a blended family or a foster or adoptive family. If the family creates a place of safety for their child, then developing resilience, independence, failing successfully, self-esteem and self-worth will be that much easier.

As mentioned before, being able to self-advocate can also support self-esteem. Accepting who you are, understanding your strengths and support needs is key to self-advocacy. That understanding of an autistic child's strengths can help to counter the negative messages they may hear in the wider world and indeed help them to be resilient and strong in their responses to those messages.

USEFUL RESOURCES FOR PARENTS OF AUTISTIC CHILDREN

WEB-BASED RESOURCES

Autism Helpline (UK)
Tel: 0845 070 4004 (open Monday–Friday, 10.00am–4.00pm)
Email: autismhelpline@nas.org.uk

Autism Self-Advocacy Network Australia and New Zealand
http://www.asan-au.org

Autism Spectrum Australia (Aspect)
(Autism non-government organisation and service provider)
www.autismspectrum.org.au

Autism Women Matter
(Audience is autistic women and, in particular, autistic women who are mothers)
http://www.autismwomenmatter.org.uk

Autistic Self Advocacy Network
http://autisticadvocacy.org

Carol Gray – Social Stories™
http://carolgraysocialstories.com/social-stories

Interoception resources
(Specific activities to develop your child's connection to themselves and others)
https://mindfulbodyawareness.com/resources

Jessica Kingsley Publishers
(Books and resources around parenting autistic children and related topics)
www.jkp.com

Positively Autistic
(Autism information and advocacy group promoting understanding around autism
    in the media and through social media and radio programmes)
http://positivelyautistic.weebly.com

Raising Children Network
(On bullying and autistic children)
http://raisingchildren.net.au/articles/bullying_children_with_autism.html

Resources at Hand
(Australian-based retailer of autism books and sensory and fidget toys)
http://www.resourcesathand.com.au/shop/index.php

SEN Assist
(Online resources for parents and teachers of autistic kids)
http://www.senassist.com/about.html

Sensory Processing Disorder Australia
http://www.spdaustralia.com.au/about-sensory-processing-disorder

Sleep Health
www.sleephealth.com.au

US Asperger and Autism Association
www.usautism.org

Visual Recipes
(Step-by-step and video recipes using photos)
http://visualrecipes.com

Yellow Ladybugs
(Australian-based advocacy and social group for girls on the autism spectrum and
    their parents)
http://yellowladybugs.com.au

BOOKS

Aitken, K.J. (2014) *Sleep Well on the Autism Spectrum.* London: Jessica Kingsley Publishers.

Brady, L.J., Gonzalez, A.X., Zawadzki, M. and Presley, C. (2012) *Speak, Move, Play and Learn with Children on the Autism Spectrum.* London: Jessica Kingsley Publishers.

Goodall, E. (2013) *Understanding and Facilitating the Achievement of Autistic Potential.* CreateSpace Independent Publishing Platform.

Grandin, T. and Moore, D. (2016) *The Loving Push.* Arlington, TX: Future Horizons.

Groden, J., Kantor, A., Woodard, C.R. and Lipsitt, L.P. (2011) *How Everyone on the Autism Spectrum, Young and Old, Can...Become Resilient, Be More Optimistic, Enjoy Humor, Be Kind, and Increase Self-Efficacy: A Positive Psychology Approach.* London: Jessica Kingsley Publishers.

Heydt, S. (2016) *A Parents' ABC of the Autism Spectrum.* London: Jessica Kingsley Publishers.

Moor, J. (2008) *Playing, Laughing and Learning with Children on the Autism Spectrum: A Practical Resource of Play Ideas for Parents and Carers,* second edition. London: Jessica Kingsley Publishers.

Murray, S. and Noland, B. (2007) *Video Modelling for Young Children with Autism Spectrum Disorders: A Practical Guide for Parents and Professionals.* London: Jessica Kingsley Publishers.

Nichols, S. with Moravcik, G.M. and Pulver Tetenbaum, S. (2009) *Girls Growing Up on the Autism Spectrum.* London: Jessica Kingsley Publishers.

Timmins, S. (2016) *Successful Social Stories™ for Young Children with Autism: Growing Up with Social Stories.* London: Jessica Kingsley Publishers.

BOOKS FOR AUTISTIC CHILDREN

Al-Ghani, K.I. (2008) *The Red Beast: Controlling Anger in Children with Asperger's Syndrome.* London: Jessica Kingsley Publishers.

Al-Ghani, K.I. (2017) *The Green-Eyed Goblin: What to Do about Jealousy – For All Children Including Those with Autism Spectrum.* London: Jessica Kingsley Publishers.

Bulhak-Paterson, D. (2015) *I am an Aspie Girl: A Book for Young Girls with Autism Spectrum Conditions.* London: Jessica Kingsley Publishers.

Elder, J. (2007) *Autistic Planet.* London: Jessica Kingsley Publishers.

Grad Gaines, A. and Englander Polsky, M. (2017) *I Have a Question about Death: A Book for Children with Autism Spectrum Disorder or Other Special Needs.* London: Jessica Kingsley Publishers.

Harrison, A.-M. (2013) *Babies are Noisy: A Book for Big Brothers and Sisters Including Those on the Autism Spectrum.* London: Jessica Kingsley Publishers.

Hoopmann, K. (2006) *All Cats Have Asperger Syndrome.* London: Jessica Kingsley Publishers.

Lindström, E. and Brunnström, Å (2017) *Robin and the White Rabbit: A Story to Help Children with Autism to Talk about Their Feelings and Join In.* London: Jessica Kingsley Publishers.

Morton, C. and Morton, G. (2015) *Why Johnny Doesn't Flap: NT is OK!* London: Jessica Kingsley Publishers.

Ochiai, M. (2005) *Different Croaks for Different Folks: All about Children with Special Learning Needs.* London: Jessica Kingsley Publishers.

Ogaz, N. (2002) *Buster and the Amazing Daisy.* London: Jessica Kingsley Publishers.

Reynolds, K.E. (2014) *Tom Needs to Go: A Book about How to Use Public Toilets Safely for Boys and Young Men with Autism and Related Conditions.* London: Jessica Kingsley Publishers.

Reynolds, K.E. (2015) *Ellie Needs to Go: A Book about How to Use Public Toilets Safely for Girls and Young Women with Autism and Related Conditions.* London: Jessica Kingsley Publishers.

Vittorini, C. and Boyer-Quick, S. (2007) *Joey Goes to the Dentist.* London: Jessica Kingsley Publishers.

Welton, J. (2005) *Adam's Alternative Sports Day: An Asperger Story.* London: Jessica Kingsley Publishers.

OTHER RESOURCES

Aspergers Parents Connect – Facebook page:
https://www.facebook.com/AspergersParentConnect

'Autism and Resilience: Are you Sure?' – Blog Post
https://jeanettepurkis.wordpress.com/2014/09/21/autism-and-resilience-are-you-sure

Autistic Motherland blog
https://autisticmotherland.com

'Disability Resilience and Achieving the Supposedly Impossible' – Presentation for TEDx Canberra by Jeanette Purkis
https://www.youtube.com/watch?v=pqdGb4TraFk

Interview by autistic author and advocate Carly Fleischmann and actor Channing Tatum
https://www.youtube.com/watch?v=a34qMg0aF6w

Sally Thibault – Autism parents newsletter, *David's Gift*
www.davidsgift.com.au

'Teaching Resilience to Children with Asperger Profiles' – published on the Asperger Autism Network site
www.aane.org/teaching-resilience-children-asperger-profiles

The Autism Show – Episode 14: 'Resilience and Independence'
http://autismshow.org/jeanette

AUTISM IN POPULAR CULTURE
Positive books about living with autism

Attwood, T. and Lesko, A. (2014) *Been There, Done That, Try This!* London: Jessica Kingsley Publishers.

Kim, C. (2014) *Nerdy, Shy and Socially Inappropriate.* London: Jessica Kingsley Publishers.

Lawson, W. (2000) *Life behind Glass.* London: Jessica Kingsley Publishers.

Regan, T. (2014) *Shorts.* London: Jessica Kingsley Publishers.

Santomauro, J. (2012) *Autism All-Stars.* London: Jessica Kingsley Publishers.

Documentaries, films, and novels

Documentary: *Alone in a Crowded Room*, directed by Lucy Paplinska, 2010.

Film: *Adam*, directed by Max Meyer, 2009.

Film: *Extremely Loud and Incredibly Close*, directed by Stephen Daldry, 2011.

Film: *Mozart and the Whale*, directed by Petter Naess, 2005.

Film: *My Name is Khan*, directed by Karan Johar, 2010.

Film: *Temple Grandin,* directed by Mick Jackson, 2010.

Novel: *The Curious Incident of the Dog in the Night-Time, Mark Haddon.* London: Vintage, 2004.

Novel: *The Rosie Project*, Graeme Simsion. New York: Simon and Schuster, 2014.

INDEX